"*Dog on my lap and driving toward Iowa...I finally had time to read your book, John. Well, my eyes are still leaking and I wiped my nose on my dog. No Kleenex anywhere. I loved it all!*"

--Cheryl Clavet, CPSN, RNFA

"*We found out the day before Thanksgiving that my wife has breast cancer. After this initial shock, we have collected ourselves and have proceeded aggressively into the 'process.' We started by talking with some friends that have been through this experience. One has written a short book on the subject from the husband's perspective. I recommend it to anyone entering into this process as one of the starting points of 'gathering your wits.' *"

--Harry See

"*I liked reading your interpretation of events. It is such an eye opener for me, the caregiver. A truly wonderful book.*"

-- Wandra K. Miles, MD

You Can't Fix Everything

By John Boyd

A Husband's Perspective On Dealing With Breast Cancer

©2010, Timber Ridge Publications
Copies available from www.amazon.com, www.createspace.com/3436952, and from www.tridgepubs.com

To Sharon, the best wife a husband could hope to know and share a life with. This book could not have been written without your abundant help, your hours of poring over the pages with your keen editorial eye, and your constant prodding me to get this done! You are without a doubt my PGOG!

This book is also dedicated to all those who provide care for loved ones actively fighting against cancer in all its forms.

Introduction

In the classic fairy tales, the young lass and handsome young man meet, fall in love, and live happily every after. In these modern times, it seems that finding the right person is for many an experiment in trial and error. But every now and then, Mr. Right meets Ms. Right, and they do fall in love, get married, and live happily ever after, against the odds. This is my story. None of the names are changed to protect the innocent (I merrily drag them along with me in this narrative).

Growing up, many guys my age and older were taught that men don't cry. Traditionally, men took out the garbage, got a job, went to work and provided for their families. Women made a house a home and stayed home to raise the children. Fortunately, my wife and I decided early on that she was more than welcome to take out the garbage or work all she wanted outside of home and hearth. We also break with tradition in that, despite not having the best housekeeping skills, I can fold laundry like a pro. We both cook but Sharon, my wife, is better at coordinating colors in the home, an area in which I admit a complete lack of ability. Sharon does most of the cleaning (to my and her relief), but when the cats bring in a four-legged "present" at all hours of the night, it's my job to capture and release it outside, earning me the fine distinction of "Chief-Executive of Things That Go Bump In The Night". Okay, so we are a bit traditional.

Yes, I know I speak in generalities, but certain roles were instilled in many of us growing up: women are nurturers and men fix things (or try to). I'm told that other men respect a man who is very handy and women love a man who repairs things. Somehow, though I'm not from a family of repairmen, I found myself embracing the traditional male role of fixing things. As a youngster, I quickly learned the difference between a metric set of tools and an SAE set. Use a power tool? Count me in! Time to get up on the roof and clean the gutters, I'm your man. Early on in college, I decided to build an entertainment center that looked great until the first electronic went into it, where it instantly developed a distinct lean to the left. My intentions and ambitions at that time greatly exceeded my abilities! I gained skills over the years that invariably spelled more work for me, but I pressed on anyway! ("Very manly," my wife tells me with an encouraging smile as she no doubt at that moment is mentally designing another project she wishes me to implement.)

I can't say that I always look forward to carrying on this fine tradition of the male in the house but hey, I'll even replace a light fixture, install a faucet or hang Sheetrock if I have to. And when my favorite tool, the computer, goes on the fritz, I run software tests or even yank out a motherboard or reset a PRAM.

As far as nurturing, well...okay...I've learned I can nurture too. When our niece, who lives with us, gets a nasty cold, I reach for some medicine, warm soup, and recommend lots of sleep. When my wife hurts her knee, I know that ice packs, anti-inflammatories, and elevation will help it.

But...what do you do when the problem is that your wife is diagnosed with breast cancer? Shortly after learning of her diagnosis, I remember seeing my trusty toolbox lying open, which struck me at that moment as a yawning cavern of utterly useless tools. And I certainly didn't have anything in my medicine cabinet that would remedy the problem in 48 hours. So while my wife goes through the struggle of dealing with the repercussions of this diagnosis...something like being unable to move out of the way of a piano falling from the sky...I stand by feeling more than a bit helpless. It's my role to fix things in my household. If I can't fix this, what good am I?

Well, the good news here is that I eventually figured out a way to help my wife, though certainly not by using Super Glue or duct tape (even though duct tape is great for just about everything else, including deep cuts—but that is another story). How? I realize that I can stand by Sharon's side, hold her hand and give her a shoulder to cry or lean on. And I can even mend my ways and actually help clean up more around the house. I can get up early to get our niece off to school, wait on my wife as needed and do jobs around the house that she normally does. And the trick is to do it all with a smile on my face. What she is going through is tough enough—I don't want her to feel any guilt for making my day harder. It's not like she partied all night and trashed the house and then ruined my car and is asking me to clean up behind her. She is not at fault here—it wasn't anything my health-conscious wife did or did not do that brought this horrible thing into our lives. With a healthy dose of optimism, maybe I can lend confidence that we'll eventually get past this hurdle and our love and our relationship will be even stronger. And maybe I can help find ways to turn this into a positive thing in our lives. This story began as a way to make sense of the shock of a potentially terminal diagnosis. This is a story of our journey, mishaps and all, and what has given us strength to get through it.

Chapter One

A True Love Story—And How Fate Stepped In

Before this story can go forward, I want to take a step backwards and tell you our story as a couple. In some ways, it's quite ordinary. In others, it's nothing short of remarkable...how events began many years ago, not so unlike multiple and different sized gears in motion so that our lives would collide together. Kind of like the contraptions Wile E. Coyote used to make on Saturday cartoons—you never really knew how the contraptions worked, only that they did and often with expected results!

Sharon grew up a tried-and-true farm girl, the youngest of six kids, outside a small town in Mississippi. At three years of age, Sharon would feel the sting of cancer as she lost her loving and dedicated mother, who was only 33 years young at the time. Growing up raised by her father, a farmer by trade, Sharon enjoyed a childhood roaming the vast acreage in and around the farm. Just seven short years later, however, Sharon lost her beloved father and moved to a city life with her grandparents. By her mid-teens, Sharon knew she would have to be independent early in life as only one grandparent remained in the home, an ailing one at that. So she managed to graduate from high school at 16 by going to summer school twice. At 17, she turned down a chance to go to college (too soon for that, she said) and worked for a year before heeding the call of adventure and travel. Relatives and friends provided many stops on the way as she traveled and looked for "adventure jobs," a prospect that seemed far more intriguing than more schooling at that time. Being an outdoors lover and the independent type, she actually preferred to camp rather than stay in motels, which were too costly anyhow on her meager budget.

Sharon was soon invited to spend the summer in Darrington, Washington, to better get to know her relatives there. Darrington's geography was as opposite to central Mississippi as you could get. Sharon joked that road cuts and bridges in parts of her home state were the tallest hills. Also in Mississippi, public access to nature preserves were too few and far between so the vast public lands in the Northwest offered

Sharon a new chapter of adventure that reminded her of the never-ending outdoor fun of her years on their private farm. Darrington, perched along the North Cascade Mountains, provided breathtaking scenery and the challenge of a true wilderness.

Her first job there was as a firewatcher atop steep mountains offering vistas that took her breath away. The Pacific Northwest's enchanting hold grew on Sharon with every visit, and after turning 18, she decided to make it her permanent home. "Grey is one of my colors," she says jokingly, referring to the backdrop of grey skies we so often see in this part of the country. From that point on, she chose to live where there were ample opportunities for biking, rafting and hiking, like Eugene, Oregon where she finished college. Now at this point you may be wondering how this has anything to do with the story, and I'll just ask your patience a bit longer. After graduating from the University of Oregon, Sharon stayed in Eugene and began working at a shelter home for troubled teens. However, fate was getting ready to deal Sharon an interesting card.

Meanwhile, my story starts in one of those small towns where if you blink more than 20,000 times, you miss it. I grew up in the suburbs of Houston, Texas. Most of my forays into "nature" as a small boy consisted of crawling through the bushes of the neighborhood, playing hide 'n' go seek, and occasional excursions into the storm sewers that ran under the streets. One excursion in the storm sewers took us about four miles away from where we started! That is, until I reached the formative age of eight, when my parents decided it was time to send me off to a true nature experience, a summer camp about two hours north of Houston called Camp Olympia. At that time, it was not what you'd call a plush camp. Most of the cabins had walls of screen and a couple of box fans in the rafters to stir the heavy humid air that came tandem with the summer heat. But camp life sparked within me a deep love of the outdoors and soon I was spending the majority of every summer there. After eight years as a camper, I made the move to camp counselor. I would end up spending 17 summers of my life at this camp, which grew into a well-known sprawling Christian sports camp perched on a 90,000-acre lake in East Texas.

I survived childhood with just the usual bumps and bruises and when time came to choose a college, I left the big city for Texas A&M. My first instinct was to major in marine biology (they also had a campus in Galveston, Texas). I grew up loving the show "Flipper" and wouldn't you know it, marine biology is directly related to what I most love to do now, but at

9

that time I followed other instincts and finished in Physical Education and Biology. I had grown to love teaching kids during my work as a camp counselor, so following a teaching pathway seemed like a path I would enjoy. Shortly after graduation, fate stepped in. I had been offered a scholarship to get a master's degree at A&M, but I had just lost my parents and was also offered a job working at Camp Olympia, my home for so many summers. The camp was in use almost 24/7 year-round with the Houston Independent School District leasing it for its outdoor education facility during the school year. My job would be to join a teaching staff of about 25 people, many of whom I knew well and who worked for both the summer camp and the school-year program at that location. Finally, after a lot of deliberation, I turned down the scholarship and opted to be near friends and in the comfort of a place I'd called home for so long.

Camp Olympia is fairly remote and draws campers and counselors from all over the world. Sharon had lived in the Northwest for 10 years, but months prior to my decision to work there, an aunt of Sharon's in Mississippi had told her about Houston's Outdoor Education Center, the nation's second-largest outdoor school. Her aunt had heard about the job through a church friend whose son worked there as a teacher.

Well, the job sounded intriguing enough to Sharon that on an infrequent visit to see relatives in Houston, she drove the two hours north to visit Camp Olympia as well. She had set up an appointment to tag along with a class in session but a massive fatal car crash on the freeway delayed her over an hour. Her tardiness forgiven, Sharon spent the rest of the afternoon touring the camp and observing outdoor classes. Her aunt was right---Houston's outdoor education program was a good match for Sharon, but the only problem was that the job wasn't in her beloved Pacific Northwest. She applied anyway but it wasn't until late summer, when she'd just finished a job in Alaska, that she was told she had been hired and that she had just a couple of weeks to show up in southeast Texas.

Despite the late-August Texas heat and humidity, mosquitoes and fire ants, my wife-to-be very reluctantly left the Northwest to take the job. For four days, she crossed the nation in her non-air-conditioned compact Toyota, begrudging the ever-growing heat, especially since she'd just spent the summer in Alaska. Sharon arrived to the usual southeast Texas heat and humidity, which she says is actually great for the skin, but the bug bites…not so much. It was too hot to eat, she says, and she actually lost 20 pounds right away, becoming as trim as she had been in high school. So the first few weeks, the jury was still out in her mind if her troubles would be worth the effort of having come so far from home and to a climate that would take some getting used to.

So fate now had our pathways converging and working together through a domino effect of seemingly random circumstances at a time in our lives when neither one of us had any interest in developing a serious relationship. Some who knew us then thought we were too different (kind of like the city mouse and country mouse) to have found enough in common. But even to our surprise, the rare combination of chemistry *and* compatibility lay waiting to be tapped....

Now you may be wondering why I'm spending so much time talking about the past in a book about dealing with the cancer. Well, some readers may see only random events colliding, but it has been my strong belief that circumstances are not wasted and any circumstance, for better or worse, can be used in a plan that ultimately benefits us...and others. A belief on this level takes faith---finding ultimate meaning in our experiences always does---but this book is inevitably also about the faith it has taken for us to get through some of those tough experiences. Before we met, we both had experienced some shattering sorrows and losses, but circumstances were unfolding to reveal how some of those events were about to serve a purpose.

It was in one of those seemingly random but fortuitous events that wound up being our first date (and an event that would ultimately have profound consequences on my life). I decided that I wanted to go to our family farm for a weekend of quiet time. Though I had never lived there (nor any of my immediate family for that matter), I had come to love this sprawling ranch as an adult, often going to mow grass and do whatever upkeep I could. Normally, I would ask "the guys," and we'd have no trouble getting a group of us to head off for a weekend of poker, famous Texas barbeque, and maybe some hunting and playing around on the three-wheelers. Well, everyone I asked that weekend had a prior commitment. On a whim that to this day I still can't explain, I asked Sharon if she would like to go. I had no ulterior motives, I promise! We had only been on group outings for pizza at that point and hardly knew each other, but I had spent plenty of weekends up on the farm by myself and just didn't feel like being alone this time. Well, Sharon thought about just the two of us being in a remote location and you can imagine what was running through her head! Her refusal was polite, and I certainly understood.

That was on a Tuesday and I made plans to go to the farm anyway but on the final night of the workweek, she passed me a note as we sat with our classes of kids at the last group campfire. The note read (to my surprise) that if it weren't too late, she'd like to change her mind. I've asked her about this quite a few times, and she can't explain why she changed her mind. Sharon had always been conservative when it came to relationships, preferring to reserve her "riskier" behavior for outdoor adventure; plus...her first impression of me as it turns out, was that I was a "womanizing good ol' boy," definitely not her type. Apparently, I had made a flippant remark weeks before to some of my buddies I've known for years about upcoming weekend plans of "cruising for chicks" (which I thought was funny since we were out in the middle of nowhere and I actually had no such plans). Anyhow, somehow I had managed to overcome that impression and we both sensed that we could trust one another enough to spend an isolated weekend on a truly remote farm.

We left on Friday afternoon for the two-hour drive into the Texas prairie. We began talking to better get to know each other and before we knew it, we were turning into the mile-long dirt road to the farm. In retrospect, I'm still amazed at the comfort level we both felt and how easily conversation came for us on that fateful weekend date exploring the farm. Little did I know when I asked her up for the weekend that she was a true farm girl and that no other surroundings could have set a more relaxed tone for our first date! We had lots of good talks, and many laughs, like the time we were on the three-wheelers and she was keeping up with me even though she was still in first gear and I was in third gear! She says she doesn't remember the high-pitched whining sound of her engine, but I do!

Anyhow, I told Sharon that one of my rules of all guests is that before they left, they had to put in one hour of chores to "pay" for their stay. She gladly spent many more hours than that tending to the neglected flowerbeds. This was another good sign to me. Again, both of us were amazed how time flew, and it was soon time to head back to camp. On the way home, I slid my hand across the Jeep console and held her hand. We ended up holding hands together the entire drive back, and after that weekend we never dated anyone else, nor wanted to.

Fifteen short months later, while on a trip to Houston with friends, it was as if a quiet voice piped up in my head, counseling me loud and clear: "You know, that Sharon is a wonderful woman. You should marry her." Without much hesitation, I figured that was a good idea, so I purchased a ring that day and made the decision to propose to her when I returned to camp later that evening. (I'm one to truly cogitate on major decisions, so the ease of this decision surprised

15

everyone---including me---that is, everyone but Sharon! How do women know these things are coming?)

I asked Sharon to marry me while sitting on a dock on Lake Livingston under the twinkling stars that evening. She didn't make things easy on me as I stammered out my unplanned proposal, and after a moment of hesitation to make me dangle a bit more, she replied, "...Okay, but just this once." From that moment forward, we were practically inseparable. Three short months later, we were married at Camp Olympia's outdoor chapel in a ceremony that had Sharon's elegant touch as well as a western casualness and even a sense of whimsy that no wedding should be without in my opinion. I decided that a western wedding theme meant I could come down the aisle with my best man to the active strains from the theme song to "The Magnificent Seven". Sharon was much more dignified, and her entrance into the chapel was a much more serene "Pachelbel Canon in D". I remember, when I turned to watch her enter the clearing and approach the alter, how the sunlight backlit her hair and made her glow. Never had I seen so beautiful a woman. My breath caught and my heart literally skipped a beat.

Officiating the wedding was a honest-to-goodness, rodeo-circuit preacher, complete with his signature handlebar mustache, his dressiest cowboy boots, bolo tie and jacket. In keeping with the western theme, after the marriage ceremony, Sharon quickly changed from her traditional wedding gown into a tailored western outfit with fringed boots to ride sidesaddle to the reception at the redecorated chow hall. I led her horse, which had been prepared for the role with ribbons braided into the mane and tail. (Hey, we Texans are proud of our western heritage and if you don't own a pair of cowboy boots soon after moving there, you're going to feel pretty left out!)

Over the years, we've lived in Texas, Oregon, and now Washington State. We have worked together for most of our marriage. We've done things that are supposed to be major stresses on couples, working side-by-side selling real estate and building, remodeling, and landscaping homes. And as the years have passed, we can easily count what most people would consider a major argument on one hand. We are lucky that though we have different personalities with often differing interests, our shared core beliefs have served as glue for our relationship.

We still sometimes laugh at the timing of our introduction. Sharon is five years older than me and the summer she turned 20, she went on her first solo cross-country drive to see her relatives in Houston. Little did she know that her future husband was a mere 14-year-old on the other side of town, probably splashing away with the neighborhood kids in the community pool. That knowledge at the time would have undoubtedly been too much to handle! Sometimes, timing is everything!

When I look back on when we first met, I'm still amazed at the odds that we met at a time when I particularly needed someone to understand what I had recently gone through. As it turns out, Sharon was the only other person our age, of a staff of 25, who knew what the early loss of both parents was like. This woman from 2200 miles away was physically, mentally, emotionally, and spiritually the woman I wanted, and more importantly, needed...though I still find it remarkable how she somehow she got this proud Texan out of sunny Texas!

The best day of my life — April 14, 1990

๛*Chapter Two*๛

Forks In The Road

As the years went by, our marriage continued to grow stronger. We had left Texas for Oregon, and then we left Oregon for San Juan Island, north of Seattle, where our sense of place and home began to grow deep roots. At first, most of our time was dedicated to building our mountain home. Once that was completed, we found work that allowed us a degree of freedom while still maintaining a moderate income. Sharon worked for a while as a property manager while I found my niche as a marine naturalist. Our lives had a sense of routine to them, and we enjoyed our lives together. We had three cats and no children (unless you count very pampered pets), so we were able to be somewhat footloose when we felt like it. We relished the fact that we could jump off the island whenever the mood hit us for a mini-vacation and to visit relatives. But too soon, we would be reminded of the specter of cancer that seemed to dog Sharon's family.

In 1996, Sharon's oldest sister, Frances, was diagnosed with breast cancer. At the time, Frances was living even more remotely than we were in a small town in New Hampshire, just minutes from the Canadian border. Frances, nine years older than Sharon, had tried to fill in a bit as a surrogate mom for her youngest sister during those first few years after losing their mother to cancer. Frances eventually moved from Mississippi to Boston, and later to New Hampshire, where she worked as a public school music teacher and played piano in restaurants and churches in her spare time. In her late thirties, Frances re-married and was excited at the prospect of finally starting a family. She had two bouncing boys right away and then a healthy daughter at the age of 43. Unfortunately, the marriage didn't work out and she was left to raise the kids and be the family provider---that is, until her diagnosis of cancer at 47. Living five hours from the nearest source for chemotherapy and radiation treatments, Frances made the decision to treat her cancer homeopathically, post-surgery, primarily by drinking carrot juice. She did well for a couple of years but the cancer came back, and Frances knew she should begin to look to extended family for someone who might take over the raising of her children.

When her health worsened, Frances made a fateful call to us, asking first Sharon and then me, that if she passed away before her children were adults, would we take them in and raise them? Sharon, having had to rely as a youngster on extended family herself, did not hesitate to say yes, but of course had to make sure I was onboard as well. I had never even met these children, and I told Frances up front that I would like some time to think about this before making a decision. I know, most people would not have hesitated to say yes to a seriously ill mother, but I wanted to think it through. I was raised that a man's word is his bond, and if I were to make this commitment, I wanted to be strong in my belief that I could follow through. After talking things over with my wife, with friends, my family and with much prayer, a week later I was able to tell Frances that I would invite her kids to live in our home if they needed us. (We had actually designed and built our home bigger, with more bedrooms than we needed, knowing this need might arise in the not-so-distant future.) Despite the doctors saying at one point that she had only a few weeks to live, Frances managed another full year, part of it in full remission and doing well, before finally succumbing to the cancer in 2005 at the age of 55.

Our experiences in raising children were limited to having only worked with kids, and we knew that becoming parent-figures in our home would alter our lives in ways that would stretch us more than perhaps any task ever had. When

Sharon's sister first asked us to consider taking her children into our home, her oldest boy was 15, the middle boy was 14, and her daughter was nine. Our home would potentially be inundated with kids and all the demands of time, money, and energy that go with it. In the end, when Frances passed, the oldest was already 18, the middle son was 17 and would be entering his senior year in high school, and the youngest was 12 and about to enter 7th grade.

When it comes to losing the ones you've most depended on, every age is a tender age. We knew that these kids needed a lot of love and patience—they had lost their mother, the only provider they had known for years, as their parents had divorced and the boys were estranged from their father. All three kids had seen their mother go from a strong, vital woman to someone who needed full-time care, and we were especially unsure of the condition of the 12-year-old daughter. Though she was a strong young lady who had stepped up to help with her mother's critical care issues---duties that no young girl should have had to endure---we didn't know the emotional condition all this might have wrought in a mere child.

Anyhow, I knew I had committed to a great responsibility and I may have gotten a few grey hairs from the experience but, as I write this several years later, I can say, happily, that our niece has blossomed into a bright, outgoing and creative young lady with a strong spirit and a thick skin. We had all three kids in our home for a brief time, but we continue to offer support and a guiding word upon need as the boys face the big wide world on their own.

Shortly after Frances's death, cancer would once again enter Sharon's life when she learned that an elderly aunt living in Lubbock, Texas, also was diagnosed with breast cancer that had metastasized to the bone. This would be Sharon's family's fourth brush with breast cancer (and, as it turned out, not nearly the last). The facts of her family history would weigh heavily on Sharon's mind.

Chapter Three

Getting The Diagnosis

As a couple, you go through the years of marriage expecting a number of ups and downs. Invariably you will have a major argument or two. Jobs are gained and lost; investments come through or fail spectacularly. For some reason, my stock portfolio never has blossomed the way I'd hoped—maybe it's because I keep buying high and selling low?

Sharon has always been what I'd call a very health-conscious person. She doesn't smoke, rarely drinks, exercises, loves plenty of fresh air, prefers lentils and tofu over red meat, won't touch soda pop—you know, one of those granola types. Early on in our marriage, I heard her being teased by her relatives as wanting to live on "pine cones" and they often offered to gather some for her. (She finally took them up on their offer and said, "If you make them taste good, I'll eat

25

them!" At this writing, she's still waiting, thankfully, for them to fulfill that dare!) Sharon also makes a point to watch the latest health trends as science learns more about what makes the body healthy or sick. With her family history, it's understandable why she'd have some concern. Starting at 36, Sharon made sure to have her annual mammograms, and would do all the checks she was supposed to. When our niece moved in, Sharon would go on and on about the importance of anti-oxidants in your diet. One day, Sharon decided we all needed to have a smoothie from fruits rich in anti-oxidants. While pouring this creamy, pink, fruit-laden smoothie into our glasses, Sharon offered a rousing spiel about combating free radicals within the body with lots of anti-oxidants. As she filled each glass to the brim with a flair, the last serving accidentally overflowed, spreading into a thick pink puddle around the base of the glass. Sharon speedily looked up at us and declared, "You know, you just can't get enough anti-oxidants!" We started laughing hysterically and it was at that moment that our niece labeled Sharon as her "Auntie Oxidant."

In the summer of 2007, while on a boating trip to a small local island, Sharon hurt her knee (I won't go into that story to save Sharon some embarrassment—let's just say her departure from our powerboat was something less than graceful). Repeated trips to the doctor uncovered what was diagnosed as severe bone bruising, micro-fractures and a torn ACL. For months, Sharon struggled with being on crutches; she says it was like having a broken leg without a cast. In the fall of 2007, we realized we had already met our deductible on our major medical insurance. (Oh, how I'm glad that I let myself get talked into health insurance!) Sharon was feeling run-down and decided to get a mammogram at just 11 months from her last one so if there were concerns (as there had been in the past with her hard-to-read films) she'd still have a bit of time for follow-up before the end of the fiscal year. So even though she had to get around on crutches, she dutifully went to the mammogram appointment at the same breast imaging office she'd gone to for years.

Unfortunately, Sharon made the trip off island but discovered that the office had erroneously dropped her mammogram appointment from the computer. The intake secretary told her to come back three weeks later for the soonest available time. So, three weeks later, the reviewing radiologist walked into the room and immediately commented, "I'm glad I'm better off than you!" She had seen my wife's crutches, but my wife didn't know that's what the comment was in reference to, seeing the doctor with her films in hand. Seeing the look of concern on my wife's face, the radiologist quickly explained. A few minutes later, the consultation ended with the doctor telling Sharon, "Your breasts are fine, go home," which Sharon did with relief. But before she arrived home from the long ferry ride, I received a call from that office stating they would like to speak with Sharon. They would give me no details and acted as if I was intruding as her husband for wanting to know what the call was about (though I am listed a contact person on her paperwork — go figure). Anyhow, when I told Sharon of this call, she didn't know what to make of it and thought if it was that important, they'd call right back. She had been called back before since dense breast tissue is very difficult to read by mammogram and areas of concern had needed another look on several occasions. All had been false alarms in the past, and when she didn't hear anything from this office for several days, she didn't think too much of it. Well, three days later, she received a call from this office and they told her to come in again because something on the mammogram indeed looked suspicious. The delays were adding up but Sharon scheduled an appointment as soon as they could see her, the following week.

Now Sharon used to dread going to any doctor, but has since met so many wonderful people in the medical profession that she has overcome the dread she routinely felt. It has been both of our experiences that most medical staff try to be thorough and kind. Sharon found, however, that some support staff members were overworked and getting critical appointments scheduled efficiently was sometimes problematic. Many patients attest to the fact that sometimes the hardest part of the exams, check-ups and re-check-ups is getting scheduled! However, we're thankful for the radiologists at that office who did take a more careful look at her difficult-to-read mammogram despite the initial "all clear." On review, while no lump was apparent, the surrounding tissue was distorted and this was indeed different from any previous concerns. At this point, we were told that distortion in surrounding tissue is viewed as very suspicious. (FYI: Many women do not know that this apparently can also result in an outward dimpling effect of the skin and if so, can often be caught by self-exam in a mirror even before the tumor can be felt.)

This development sounded different to Sharon as well, so it was with a bit of trepidation that she went back again for more tests. Well, after a month of delays, Sharon really wanted to know what the radiologist had to say about the suspicious spot. On her return visit, still unclear as to what they were looking at, the radiologists performed an ultrasound and biopsy on the spot. (I had to quiz Sharon on the details on this as I'm a guy and somewhat ignorant in the ways of "women stuff.") She said that if cancer is detected, the usual protocol is to send all films and info to the initial examining doctor, perhaps a woman's gynecologist, or to the physician who had been the referring doctor for mammograms in the first place. (Sharon's breast tumor could not be felt and had been missed by a hands-on examination at the gynecologist's office a few weeks earlier.)

Well, when the patient is lying there being scanned and the radiologist sees a definite problem, he or she has the dilemma of saying nothing or saying too much about what their trained eye is telling them, but due to the delays and to cumbersome travel, Sharon wanted the truth and pressed for it. It was at this appointment that Sharon learned that she too probably had cancer, both by the radiologist's demeanor and the comment, "I hope you like broccoli." Sharon at that point knew the "menu tip" wasn't in reference to the upcoming Thanksgiving dinner the following week.

(As an aside, the technology is out there and word needs to get out more about the value of MRIs for women with dense breast tissue and a family history of breast cancer. The year prior, Sharon had asked that same imaging office if she could get an MRI, worried as she was about family history. She was told in abrupt fashion, "Oh, that isn't done yet." The scheduler was in a hurry and Sharon had only read of the technology and assumed that it must be rare, when in fact she could have been referred to Seattle months prior to her diagnosis. With slow growing cancers, such as hers, perhaps it might have been detected at an earlier stage, but this is not known and we do not wish to over-speculate now. We of course wish we had known she could have gotten a breast MRI months earlier but the timing was what it was. Yes, it would have been expensive, but the choice would have been ours.

After the Thanksgiving holidays, Sharon's gynecologist called her at home after having reviewed her films and test results. Nearly five weeks had passed since her initial dropped-from-the-computer appointment. She happened to be home alone that day and, again, Sharon could guess the outcome from the gravity of the doctor's tone. She requested confirmation right then and there rather than make another off-island trip just to get the official news in person---understandably, the preferred protocol.

I remember the tearful call shortly after she received the news. I ache now thinking that I wasn't at home to comfort her, to give her a shoulder to cry on. For me, it was at this point in our experience that I began to see little glimmers that no matter how much you hope life will go smoothly with no glitches, the going gets rocky. And when it comes to medical care, there will inevitably be time delays of one kind or another with imperfect logistics built into office "machinery," i.e. office and insurance paperwork, availability of appointments, overworked personnel, strict protocols, etc. Diagnostics and treatments can never be fast enough for the worried patient and for his or her loved ones. In the midst of exasperating delays and a near miss at the diagnosis, we forged ahead at our next task to choose a hospital and surgeon who would operate on Sharon and help dictate the rest of her health...and life.

Sharon knew she had to pick a surgeon and hospital as quickly as possible, which she did after an afternoon of a few phone calls. We knew no surgeons nor did we have a physician-referral, which is customary, but Sharon's gynecologist did not have a working relationship with any surgeons at Swedish Hospital in Seattle, her choice for hospitals. Sharon really wanted to go to the big city for something of this magnitude and was guided by Seattle's very patient-oriented Swedish Hospital staff to a surgeon named Dr. Christine Lee. Sharon was assured that Dr. Lee was a very no-nonsense doctor whose expertise was among the very best. A few days later, Sharon, being the independent type, thought she could handle driving herself to her first appointment to consult with her choice of surgeons at Seattle's acclaimed Swedish Medical Center. I had a scheduling conflict and she decided to go alone rather than ask a friend. How I wish I had cleared my schedule to take her as she had too much time alone to dwell on her fate in view of the ominous fact that she had lost three close relatives to breast cancer, two in the last two years.

Perhaps the steady dreary rain of that day contributed to Sharon's mood sinking lower and lower. On the drive home, she particularly couldn't get out of her head her sister's battle, one she had seen firsthand. I called her when she was negotiating Seattle traffic between tears and rain, and I became worried that she was in no condition to drive and wouldn't make it back home. Her words, that I thankfully never heard her repeat again, were, "If I did die in an accident, I'd rather die that way anyway."

I rushed to assure Sharon that diagnostics were much better than when her sister was diagnosed; that by going to Swedish Hospital, she was getting the latest treatments from the finest doctors; and that her healthy diet and lifestyle in general gave her added advantage. I also assured her (and still tell her all the time) that I am here to support her every step of the way because I want her around a long time! But, wow--- watching from the house that evening for her headlights to turn into our driveway was one of the longest waits I've ever experienced. You can't imagine how much I wanted to be there with her and I determined right then that I would attend every appointment possible from then on.

Guys, let me tell you, if you love your wife---and if you are reading this book, you must---there are few things in life more important than just being available to her. You may feel like you are useless just sitting there for the routine appointments (there will be many) and you may spend most of your time reading magazines you hope your friends don't catch you reading in the waiting room. (I don't know why more women's doctors don't have the latest in *Car & Driver*, *Off-Roader*, *Sports Illustrated*, *Macho Tool Guy Magazine* and such.) I just know that when I have held my wife's hand while she discussed the more difficult matters with her doctors, or when I offered an appropriate (hopefully not too lame) joke when things seemed tense, these simple things meant all-the-world to my wife. Another straightforward reason to be at your wife's appointments is so you can hear firsthand what the doctors are saying. You may catch useful facts and instructions otherwise missed as the patient's ongoing mild state of shock from this kind of diagnosis can hinder one's ability to absorb a lot of new information.

So I began making the trips to Seattle with Sharon. I began learning the lingo of the oncology world. I learned the difference between malignant and benign tumors. I won't get into the gist of all of it, but you begin to understand why a Stage Zero is better than Stage One, and what is the difference and importance of considering a lumpectomy versus a mastectomy. I paid attention to what the doctor said so I could later respond intelligently when my wife asked me for details or clarification, as she often did. Two sets of ears definitely catch more when listening to what can sound like a foreign language.

Dr. Lee, Sharon's surgeon, had told her at her first consult that an MRI was needed next, as well as a battery of other tests and that her office would help expedite these many appointments. Swedish Hospital's secretaries and doctors worked with us to double up on doctor appointments the same day to limit trips on the 6 a.m. "red-eye" ferry only to return home well after dark. (All right, a game plan—perhaps involving lots of transportation but something I can help with and feel like I'm doing something to fix this). So the next week, I drove my wife to Seattle to see an MRI specialist to get a better idea of what we were working against.

Dr. Porter is an MRI radiologist with a very soft-spoken approach, but one who carries a lot of clout. Turns out he is one of the most highly respected radiologists in his field in the entire world. He travels around the world teaching others how to use MRIs to detect breast cancer (a diagnostic development in the last few years that is saving lives). Sharon and I feel fortunate to have caught him between trips, and he also tells us he is going to retire soon from the patient side of things so he can teach and travel more. We are grateful for having been referred to such competent hands. After being scanned every which way, Sharon emerged from the examining room at Dr. Porter's office as the workday was coming to a close. Dr. Porter graciously said that if we didn't mind waiting a bit longer, he could actually give us a preliminary analysis of the MRI findings (this often takes a day or two longer). Of course we were willing to wait and after about an hour, we were ushered into a conference room. After a bit of small talk (and finding out that wives named Sharon are the best---Dr. Porter and I will attest to that), we got to the task at hand. On the wall is a projection of Sharon's MRI, and in one breast is a bright lump with jagged edges, the suspicious kind. But Dr. Porter was very positive and said things looked as good as they can— it's a small (2 cm) lump with defined margins, but Dr. Porter was concerned as Sharon has very dense breast tissue and there are a few other spots that also had him worried. Dense tissue is very hard to read even with MRIs, but MRIs in the hands of trained professionals are very thorough and this research has revealed that oftentimes, more than one tumor is present. Dr.

Porter wanted to do a few more biopsies, but he had another patient due any minute, his last appointment of the day. We would need to come back to Seattle for an accurate diagnosis on the additional areas of concern. More very nerve-wracking time delay, allowing the dread to build in both our minds about just how bad things might reveal to be....

But then a small miracle...as we were getting ready to leave, Dr. Porter's last appointment of the day calls in to cancel. We were quickly informed that due to this unexpected last-minute cancellation, more biopsies could be taken right then and there, including lab results, if we were interested in staying for that as well. In the end, several technicians ended up staying late for Sharon and we are still amazed at how caring and sacrificial of their evening plans everyone was, especially Dr. Porter, who cancelled his formal dinner plans. In the kindest and most caring way at Dr. Porter's office, we were told that the four other areas of suspect, though all quite small, are also cancers.

So there we were, rocked to our cores, with our brains reeling at the implications. It's times like this, I think, that it's easy to go along in life thinking we're in control, until things happen that show us how silly that notion really is. How bad is it? Has it spread beyond the breast? Oh no, am I going to lose my wife? Oh God, why is this happening?

Imaging appointments and biopsies happen early in the process and patients are still just trying to digest what is happening to them. We were told that this Seattle imaging center sees three or four new breast cancer cases *every week*. Truly a tough job but one, we found, executed with much sensitivity and genuine concern. But this is also where our faith had to kick in. As we sat there hours from home and while we were overwhelmed at this next course of news, we were struck with an amazing set of coincidences--*what if* Sharon hadn't hurt her knee? Would she have put off her mammogram a few more months as she was thinking of doing before we reached our deductible? When her usual mammogram office dropped her first appointment from their computer, *what if* Sharon, still hobbling about on crutches and out of frustration of going off island solely for her dropped appointment, had succumbed to the temptation again of putting off the appointment months further out? Instead, she did comply and went back three weeks later, the soonest the scheduler could find another opening. *What if* the mammogram radiologists had missed the vague distortion of film and hadn't asked Sharon to come back in? *What if* Sharon hadn't been scheduled for an MRI from one of the top imaging doctors in the region, even in the world, thanks to her surgeon's recommendation at Swedish? Again, the technology was relatively new at the time. Needless to say, the list of *"what ifs"* amaze us. While every step of the way had not gone perfectly, things could have been much worse. We believed that God was hearing our prayers even amidst the chaos of events out of our control. Finally, the diagnosis was certain and treatments could begin. We would find out later, of course, only from surgery, if the cancer had spread further than the breast.

From that point on, an intense round of appointments began. They say that love gives us wings, and that we will do some crazy things for the ones we love. Love can make you stand up for your spouse, this I know, and with a little help, you can get some things done you never expected. For example, a couple of weeks into our travels back and forth to the mainland for appointments, we encountered a hitch in our transportation plans.

Sharon and I had different commitments off-island. Sharon was still hobbling around on one crutch but managed to combine some needed Christmas shopping with a follow-up doctor appointment. We were planning to meet onboard the same ferry in Anacortes to head home and I at least would ride the last two hours home with my wife. I was already onboard when my cell phone rang. It was Sharon, sounding chagrined. She called to say that even though the ferry wasn't scheduled to leave the dock for five more minutes, the terminal crew wouldn't let her load her car. She had been told she had cut it too close, although the ferry was far from full and had not yet left the dock. We had never encountered this situation before with the ferry system, often able to tag in at the last minute during the off-season...but security concerns are always making the rules tighter. Anyhow, I ran to the upper deck to see what was going on, and I could see her car in the ferry parking lot, the sole car in line for the next ferry, several hours later.

Keep in mind that it's cold—this is the third week of December by now and I could clearly see there was plenty of room on the ferry. I gave a shout to the crew that they were leaving my wife behind, and they graciously called the workers at the terminal, but it had already been decided not to load my wife, especially since by that point, only two minutes remained until departure time. As we pulled off the dock, I stepped outside, watching my wife alone in her car in 40-degree weather, and something inside me said this wasn't right. I went back inside to talk to the crew once again. I explained that my wife was on crutches (okay, just one crutch at that point unless using stairs), that she had just recently found out she had breast cancer, that she happened to be my ride home once we arrived to our island, but most of all that I really didn't think it was a good time for her to be alone for several hours. Sure, she had cut it close, but she had seen the last car drive on and for some reason, she was told she couldn't.

Well, I must have been pretty convincing, as the purser (head of the deck crew) called up to the captain, and soon, I felt the boat slow to a stop and actually begin its way back to the ferry dock to load my wife! I've never witnessed a ferry going back for a customer, but on this day they did. This "ship," capable of carrying 200 cars, had gotten well away from the dock but turned around for my wife---about a 15 minute process to stop, reverse, and *wait for a small ferry to unload before being able re-dock and load Sharon's car.*

My eyes began to tear up as I made my way to the car deck to check on my wife. She was a bit embarrassed by the whole thing, but thankful she was able to make the ride home with me. We found the purser and thanked both him and the captain profusely, especially as this was no small ferry. Apparently, love can even turn ships around! I will always be thankful to the Washington State Ferry boat crew for their compassionate decision that day. Thanks again to J-Watch crew, chiefly the Captain!

Later in the week, when that same crew arrived in Friday Harbor, I was waiting with a huge basket of home-baked goodies. We had never baked so much at one time. After that, we learned in quick order the steps necessary to get an official priority loading for the duration of Sharon's treatments. Most crews seemed to recognize us and were glad to make sure we were parked near the elevator.

Chapter Four

The Surgeon & Pre-surgery Decisions

When it comes to surgery, I try to avoid it whenever possible. I had dual knee surgery in 1984, and was stuck in a room for a week by myself well before the age of a gazillion channels on cable. So to me, the word surgery is definitely on the "avoid-if-possible" list! There are many kinds of surgeries, but to me, cancer surgeries seem so unreal and somewhat unfathomable.

Sharon (and I, to a small degree) had to navigate the maze of surgical procedures and options available to her. It is here again that we felt reassurance of a guiding hand in our choices. Many other doctors went out of their way to compliment Sharon's choice of surgeons and their sincere praise helped bolster her confidence that she indeed had made a wise choice with Dr. Christine Lee. After their first meeting,

Sharon said that Dr. Lee was very smart and sure, but at first blush, seemed a bit clinical. But that was okay, as Sharon added quickly, since no-nonsense, objective and qualified are what you want in a surgeon! Later in December when we both had a chance to sit with Dr. Lee and discuss our surgical options, I caught glimpses of humor behind the highly honed professional demeanor. I was instantly struck by how assured Dr. Lee was of what needed to be done and how she would help coordinate Sharon to see other specialists, a task she had already begun with the referral to the MRI specialist, Dr. Porter. Dr. Lee further informed us how a team of doctors, radiologists, oncologists and plastic surgeons, get onboard for a diagnosis of this nature. I felt better already. I liked having a game plan that made sense to me and by keeping all her doctors under one roof, in a facility as big as Swedish, Sharon began to notice how the chain of communications between doctors was much more expedient—they all had working relationships with each other and could walk to consult with each other, if need be.

After discussing with Dr. Lee the options of lumpectomy versus mastectomy, and taking into consideration Sharon's family history, it was decided that the best option for a long, healthy life would be for Sharon to have a bilateral mastectomy (removal of soft tissue and all ductal material in both breasts). Sharon had already accepted that this course would be the best and she had already been told that reconstruction is covered by insurance in the case of a mastectomy. Though she struggled with the feeling of loss and fear of unknown reconstructive issues, Sharon actually wanted the double mastectomy, the sooner the better. However, I was touched how Sharon was concerned about how I would take it, and I told her that having her alive was more important to me than the loss of her breasts.

But before her surgery could happen, many, many lab tests had to be scheduled. There were blood tests, PET scans, CAT scans and bone density scans (don't I sound all technical?). During all this, I felt I was part of the solution--- to help mind the schedule, drive to the appointments and help keep track of information accumulated during each appointment. Most importantly, I kept reminding my wife how important she is to me, and that no matter what, she is a beautiful woman. I am quite fortunate in that my work is seasonal from April to late October, so the timing of Sharon's most critical care allowed me to be at most appointments, and also to be her "nurse" at home after surgery.

It seems that more and more men are seen in doctors' waiting rooms with the special women in their lives. While close friends and relatives can of course help, I wasn't sure I wanted a substitute to accompany my partner in life during these difficult appointments. I figured that just being there sent a message of acceptance and support from the person she needed it from most. (We would find out at a later clinical trial interview what a difference it might have made had I been in the exam room during a trying appointment to help soften harsh news.)

Okay, at this point I can only draw conclusions based on my experiences and biases, but I cannot begin to tell you how important it is for a husband to let his wife know that he truly believes that the removal of one or both breasts will not turn her into an unattractive woman. Women are very conscious of their figure (and guys are conscious of it too even if they only admit that they look only at a woman's eyes) and your wife is going to be very sensitive about this surgery. Though some do not opt for reconstructive surgery, the prospect of this helped keep Sharon's spirits up. I admit also that the prospect of reconstruction lent a final note of normality back to the whole ordeal. (A historical note of thanks to Senator Alfonse D'Amato (R-NY) and Representative Sue Kelly (R-NY) whose efforts helped to pass legislation in 1998 to put reconstructive surgery after breast cancer surgery under general care for insurance purposes.)

For me, I have always relied on humor to help me deal with stress. But breast cancer is nothing to joke about and at times, I had to reel in my penchant to crack a joke to lighten the mood. On top of the sensitive and scary health aspects, who wouldn't feel very vulnerable about appearance-altering surgery?

One aspect of this process we could joke about, thankfully, was reconstruction options. We were told a story of a basically flat-chested woman who had a double mastectomy and who was looking forward to going "shopping" for a chest size that she felt would fit her frame and personality. During the reconstructive phase, she remarked how soon she'd have the "boobs of a 20 year-old" and she personally appreciated the option to have something much greater than nature had ever given her. In Sharon's case, she felt the opposite. Having a little less than nature had given her was preferred and this option gave her something to look forward to.

During consults with her plastic surgeon, my wife continued to discover more of the bright side to reconstruction options with many surgeons using natural tissues when possible to replace the breast tissues. Some women end up with a "free" tummy tuck and others may get a "free" eye-lift for use of that soft skin elsewhere. There are many strategies to be considered and some of them have pleasant side benefits. Taking excess from the body in one place to rebuild what was lost is an idea my wife thinks is brilliant! Hooray for the surgeons who thought of that, as this certainly wasn't always the case with mastectomies.

With an appointment or two every week, we eventually dotted every "i" and crossed every "t" to prepare for the first operation. The mastectomy surgery date was marked on the calendar and at times a quick glance at it made me feel as if we were facing D-Day. Sharon had experienced anesthesia and surgery only once while having her wisdom teeth removed in a dental office, and now she was facing a major surgery that would take away part of her body and would determine if the cancer might have traveled into lymph nodes. I had to mentally check myself and remind my brain that this surgery was intended to save the life of someone I loved more than anything, and that it was this date that would rid my wife of cancer and add back the years that an untreated cancer would take away. If a mastectomy could do that, then all that remained was where and when!

One of Sharon's nurses had told her of a breast cancer patient (of course no names were given) who had recently cancelled her surgery for a double mastectomy on the day of surgery itself. Let me just say that, frankly, while I greatly appreciated my wife's double D breasts over the years, I was glad that wasn't my wife who changed her mind.

৵*Chapter Five*ॐ

Surgery (Kids, Don't Try This At Home)

Thanksgiving and Christmas of 2007 had come and gone with an undercurrent of fear and trepidation though, at the time, we tried hard to put on a cheerful face for all the social gatherings. As the year came to a close in wait for surgery in January, you could feel the somber mood in our home. It was a trying time, I must confess. The usual light laughter I had grown accustomed to around our house hadn't been heard in quite a while.

The mood had a somber tone but as a couple, we had always been outwardly affectionate. Now we were especially so, sitting close and holding hands every chance we got. Like couples newly in love and who cherish every moment together, the magic of a renewed deep appreciation for each other was palpable for both of us. Even just touching feet while catching some "couch time" and watching TV was treasured time.

Weeks had passed since Sharon's diagnosis and when it came to telling relatives, she was hesitant to let them know that yet another family member was faced with the life-threatening problem of breast cancer. Being a private person, Sharon tells me that she would not initially have been as forthcoming to acquaintances and friends at large about her diagnosis. But since I am naturally open about sharing concerns, she adds that she was glad for the support we both received (something I didn't think about, but in retrospect, I needed the support too). In being open, we found that most people want to show genuine concern and sensitivity and because better treatments and outcomes are making a sensitive subject a little more approachable, these matters aren't nearly as hard to talk about as they were even a decade ago.

But we didn't tell everyone. Sharon decided to keep her diagnosis secret a bit longer from her remaining four siblings who lived in other states. While I thought she would benefit from their support, I left this decision to her, since she continued to insist on not putting her siblings through another scare of all the unknowns at that point if she didn't have to. She would have immediately told her remaining sisters if her genetics test, which also had been recommended early on by Dr. Lee, had turned out positive for the two genes doctors now recognize as causing breast cancer. We thankfully discovered that Sharon did not have those genes so her sisters were unlikely to either. We were told, however, that there was undoubtedly a familial connection in Sharon's case but current science can't yet identify which genes, beyond the two now known for breast cancer potential, put women at greater risk.

As a digression, the odds factor in the U.S. is that 80% of new breast cancer cases occur in families with no history of the problem. And studies have shown that in only two generations of having moved to the U.S., Asian and Latino women catch up to the rest of the population here with breast cancer risks. Clearly, something environmental or a complex combination of things is very wrong. Another reason to follow every preventative guideline that we do know, says my wife. (Some common plastic food and water containers and even parabens found in many cosmetics are suspect!)

Most of us know which foods stand out more than others as problematic but as a reminder, a list of things to avoid follows: processed (highly manipulated) food with additives for long shelf life, saturated fats, and of course, trans-fats. Also, avoid foods with high sugar content and little fiber, a combination that spikes blood sugar---and cancer cells love sugar. Something we hear less about is exposure to pollutants in household cleaners and, as briefly mentioned, even in body lotions with ingredients that act as xenoestrogens, substances that have a magnifying estrogen effect in both men and women and which can contribute to both breast cancer and prostate cancer risks.

Of course, healthy fresh produce free of pesticides and herbicides is seen as helpful in preventing and fighting cancer. Doctors also know to recommend regular exercise, especially stress reducing deep-breathing exercises, as well as plenty of fresh air and sunshine. We need that vitamin D!

Perhaps no one factor, not even genes, can be singled out as at fault. Many researchers believe that a genetic disposition for the disease still has to be acted on by the environment to develop into disease. For that reason, Sharon had avoided a lot of problem environmental ingredients for years---she used vinegar and baking soda for most of the housecleaning and we have hand-weeded our extensive landscaping beds for 20 years to avoid polluting the soil and groundwater. Perhaps research will soon make great strides in putting the puzzle pieces together as to the cumulative environmental factors causing this epidemic problem in countries such as ours. In Sharon's case, she may have inherited a propensity toward the problem but the alarming fact is that cases are showing up at younger and younger ages and in families with no history of breast cancer. Of course, as mentioned above, both women and men can be proactive to a large degree about what we expose ourselves to. But enough for the research speculations for now....

Well, here it was time for major surgery and the only relatives Sharon had told were cousins whom we saw fairly often and who would have found out anyhow. Of course our 14-year-old niece who lived with us knew, and Sharon was determined to show this niece, who had lost her mom to breast cancer, that a patient of this disease can be assertive in getting every treatment available that the experts recommend. Sharon is one to research her options and she heavily relied on the doctor-written website *www.breastcancer.org* to answer questions and to help her ask more informed questions of her own doctors. Still, she wanted to be armed with more information about her diagnosis, treatments, and a bit on how she would physically respond herself--before telling her siblings. I went along with this as another way to support her wishes.

My wife was slated to have her surgery on January 2nd, 2008. So as New Year's Eve approached, we took every opportunity to spend time together, trying not to dwell too much on the events of the next day. Hospitals did not hold good memories for Sharon with the early deaths of her parents. She had lost many relatives while they lay in hospital beds, especially her father, whom she adored, confined to a hospital bed by a broken hip and a history of heart problems. Though his hip was mending nicely, his heart gave out after two weeks of inactivity. Sharon remembered him complaining of major digestive problems from hospital food, and her 11-year-old mind at the time managed to put some of the blame of her father's death on what he was fed. At least the adult Sharon could see through fear of death by hospital food!

But of course Sharon was not immune to the usual big concerns of a major surgery and always on her mind was that pesky question: Would they find cancer in the lymph nodes? She also had to deal with questions of whether she would feel less feminine or attractive. While Sharon was looking forward to having any cancers removed, the figure-altering aspect felt like an amputation to her. But again, the prospect of reconstruction went a long way in granting my wife something to look forward to after the "demolition" phase of her treatment---her words for describing that portion of the process. Yes, she too utilized a bit of humor to cope with the enormity of what she must face.

On New Year's Day, while most people were recovering from their revelry, I got up early to make a lunch of black-eyed peas and cornbread. Sharon has never met a vegetable she doesn't like and eating black-eyed peas on New Year's Day is a Southern tradition thought to bring luck. Besides choosing a vegetable we both liked, I figured we'd take every bit of psychological boost we could muster. (Seasoned right, black-eyed peas truly are very tasty, especially with my favorite recipe of homemade cornbread!)

Later that afternoon, we drove to Seattle to spend the night just blocks from Swedish Hospital so we could get there without any major hassles bright and early the next morning. We were fortunate to have family from the mainland free to come to the island to housesit for us for several days and to make sure our niece got to school and ate real food. This would also ensure that our niece would have the reassurance of family members during a difficult few days. And so, with packed bags, we headed out on to catch a ferry to Anacortes, then on to Seattle to stay in the most convenient hotel, as Sharon's double mastectomy was scheduled at 7 a.m. the next day.

Now normally, Sharon and I argue very little. But I could tell that Sharon was tense, so I felt I'd better watch my "P's and Q's" during the long drive to Seattle. Smile, be supportive and just hunker down and be there for my wife and we'll do fine on the long drive, I coached myself. Mostly, I sang. I had made a CD of tunes that I knew Sharon liked as well and for nearly two hours, I serenaded my wife with some easy-listening rock. (I like to think it was closer to serenading and not tortured warbling.) Later, she told me that this was the most supportive thing I could have done. It soothed those ravaged nerves over so many unknowns. She knew the surgery was to free her of cancer but one can understand the need for soothing music, to say the least! She still can't listen to James Taylor ballads without getting misty-eyed, she tells me, as his songs will always remind her of how I chose to distract her on that long drive in the dreary rain to Seattle. I won't win any singing contests, but it worked to calm and distract her!

The morning of the surgery, Sharon was up early and ready to go. We had been instructed to be at the hospital promptly at 7 a.m. We were staying at a hotel only a few blocks away but since we didn't know exactly where the surgical check-in wing was, we were a bit nervous about arriving on time. The hotel staff assured us the night before that the hotel shuttle went directly to the correct location all the time and would get us there in plenty of time for Sharon's 7 a.m. appointment. Sharon, by that time felt this was the most important appointment in her life, second to being on time for our wedding (which she wasn't on time for---to my growing trepidation but, in fairness, her ride wasn't there on time---a problem she did not want to repeat)!

In my wife's mind, any additional delays were not welcome. It had now been close to three months since the initial mammogram appointment she had scheduled in October, only to have it cancelled on her, which had caused subsequent appointments to run into all the major holiday delays. Well, we waited several more minutes and when the driver was unfortunately not ready as promised, it looked like we would have to get ourselves to the surgical check-in desk. Silly us, we still had no idea where to go, as all our appointments had been in other wings of a hospital that covers several city blocks. Well...guys, it's really important to remember that you may get hollered at in the process of figuring out your next step so you won't be late but trust me—the touchy nerves are not directed at you. Frayed nerves on the morning of surgery can easily be stretched and broken. In this event, you will have to fight the urge to counter back. Knowing we were running late, Sharon's tearful plea was, "I just need to get this over with!" To do something, anything, to remedy the situation, I ended up grabbing an umbrella from the hotel's front desk. The two of us beat a path the few blocks uphill, with Sharon ignoring the shelter of the umbrella and rushing past me (though she was just days fully off both crutches and still with a touchy knee). I caught up to her and off we tromped in the early morning drizzle to an entry we knew, getting lost in a maze of long corridors.

We finally arrived at what we later found to be a quite easily located desk, had we not been under such stress and had scouted it out before. Ah---the old adage---hindsight is everything. Suffice it to say, that walk seemed like the longest walk of our lives, though we were only about 10 minutes late. (When the hotel management found out what had happened soon thereafter, the manager apologized profusely and assured us it would never happen again. We have since stayed there and been treated with the utmost professional courtesy one could find.)

Surgery check-in is yet another fine example of how complicated life can be. First there is the line to verify your identity and method of payment. Then they send you to another line to check in for surgery. It's the classic "hurry up and wait" system, but we were fortunate that the hospital had this routine down well and our wait wasn't too terribly long. But as you wait, it's hard not to over-think about all the things you are already worried about, making the situation even more traumatic. We both have to compliment Seattle's Swedish Hospital for their courteous staff who day after day deal with wide-eyed newbies like us, trying to put us more at ease.

Soon we were ushered into a large staging area with curtained cubicles for changing. First is the gown with the open back end that shows off your rear when you walk around. But quick thinking (and a lot of experience) had the hospital staff also providing bottoms and even a robe so that no body part that shouldn't be displayed wasn't exposed for the world to see. The process of pre-surgery readiness strips one of all the extraneous things (no makeup, no jewelry, no street clothes, no food/drink the previous 8-12 hours and finally, no corrective lenses). You are given an information band on your wrist, and every single doctor, nurse, surgeon, etc. checked the band and re-confirmed the surgery type and location (causing me to snicker to myself---these were Sharon's doctors, didn't they KNOW what they were doing?). Again, being there by Sharon's side was very important as I listened to the torrent of instructions and questions each person asked. It can be a confusing jumble as people come and go, bringing in equipment to draw blood and check vital signs, asking for signatures and so forth, but staying busy is better than "hurry up and wait." Things were starting to relax a bit. Just an hour or so before, we'd been beyond stressed about where to find the check-in desk so as not to delay her surgeons, or worse case scenario, lose a hard-to-get operating room time slot, as we weren't sure how tight the scheduling was in her circumstance.

Now keep in mind the pre-op changing room was full, and that the "walls" were made of fabric. As I said, I deal with stress with humor, and anytime I can make Sharon laugh is good for me. So my mind wandered to places beyond good taste as I made up dramatized scenarios how her surgeons might react if she passed gas loudly while under anesthesia. I'm reluctant to admit that a little tasteless humor was just the ticket for us in those circumstances. Maybe it was the overwrought nerves, as the idea doesn't seem so funny now--- but it did the trick then as we were both laughing so hard our stomachs began hurting. Our neighbors behind the curtain walls must have thought we were 12, but that's okay. The sight of Sharon smiling and the sound of her laughter were well worth it.

Soon you are in the pre-op room and you get a moment of silence. Sharon is about to take her first step of actual breast cancer treatment after what turned out to be months of diagnostic tests. You think to yourself, things are going to be okay, right? You review in your mind: I've done all I can and the surgeons are going to do everything as perfectly as they can. There was a bit of hovering, I admit, and lots of hand-holding as Sharon lay in the bed they would soon roll into the operating room.

When the doctors came in for the last time, they reviewed with us the procedures for the bilateral mastectomy. I was told it was about a five-hour surgery, an hour and a half for recovery, and then Sharon would be moved to her room. So after last-minute hand holding, a quickly whispered prayer, a big hug and a few tears from both of us, the orderlies, surgeon, and anesthesiologist wheeled Sharon into surgery, and I began the process of waiting....

I remember watching the gurney being wheeled away from me as it pushed past large double doors and I offered up yet another prayer to God that all would go well and that I would soon see her smiling face again.

When Sharon was wheeled into surgery, it was 9:30 a.m. Being the great mathematician that I am, I figured that she'd be done at 2:30 p.m. So I wandered around the hospital for a while, figuring out where everything was. I wanted to be prepared to meet any of Sharon's needs, whether it was for a smoothie (full of anti-oxidants!) or just another pillow for her bed. Soon the wandering lost its appeal so I headed back to the hotel, making sure that the hospital had my hotel number, my cell phone number, and even my wife's cell number, since I had that phone too. At 11:30 a.m., I got a call from the anesthesiologist in the operating room letting me know that so far everything was looking really good. Around 1:30, I figured it was time to mosey back to the hospital's waiting area, so I'd be ready to spring to my wife's side when she woke up. Upon my return to the waiting room, I was issued a pager that would light up and beep when the desk had any information for me.

Time kept passing, and other families waiting in the lounge came and went. I sat patiently watching the images on daytime television (people actually watch that stuff?) and I began to get a bit concerned when 4:00 p.m. came and still no word. I kept checking my beeper to make sure it was working. I began to think the worst when I was finally paged, at 4:30, that Dr. Lee was on her way down. She must have seen the concern on my face as she approached, as she looked at me and then smiled a big smile. In my brain, I replayed every episode of ER, House, Doogie Howser, Marcus Welby, MD (yes, I'm old enough to remember the show) and I came up with the following formula:

Surgery (Kids, Don't Try This At Home)

☹ *frowning doctor=bad news*
☺ *smiling doctor=good news*

I could barely hold in my relief that the surgery went perfectly. Dr. Lee apologized for the delay, as extra time was needed to do a thorough and complete job. The job was more than just removing breast tissue---it also meant making sure the skin was in good condition for the reconstructive surgeries to come, as well as removing lymph nodes to check for any cancer there.

Well, I was told that the initial prognosis was good news---all cancers removed from the breasts and no visible cancer in the lymph nodes! Praise be to God, I thought to myself, as I hugged Dr. Lee. My hug surprised her but broke the ice from then on, allowing me insight beyond the classic hard-driving, young professional---to someone that I knew did her job first for the sake of helping people.

I was told Sharon was doing great but it would be a bit longer before I'd be allowed to go up to see her, so I took the time to call my family to let them know the good news. The first call to my "little" brother, now in his forties as well, was hardly more than a whisper as I cried while trying to leave a message. But I was able to get in control of my emotions better by the fifth and sixth calls to other family members!

After what seemed an eternity, I was given Sharon's room number, and I made my way up to see her. I was pleasantly surprised to see that not only was Sharon up, but pretty coherent as well. I was amazed that after seven hours of surgery, she was sitting up and talking. She would drift to sleep occasionally for a few minutes, but then she'd wake up and we'd talk more. The hardest part of waiting for her to wake up between her deep naps was that the television didn't have Tivo, so I'd suffer the commercials in silence (hey, no sacrifice is too small for my sweetheart!).

During the surgery process, you don't get to form what I'd call "happy memories." But when Sharon came back to consciousness, I was able to deliver great news. Sharon did not know the outcome of her surgery, so I was the one to tell her that they had successfully removed all the cancers in her breasts, and that the lymph nodes had no visible tumors in them. We smiled, cried and thanked God together in the flickering light of the television. (I'm secure enough in my masculinity that I can admit I cried yet again!) I stayed in the hospital for as long as they'd let me, until the staff finally kicked me out at 9:00 p.m. I had the chance to meet all the staff nurses and, after writing my contact information on the dry erase board for them, I kissed Sharon on the head and made my way back to the hotel to get some sleep. It took me quite awhile to unwind from the stresses of the day and fall asleep. Just as I was drifting off, my phone rang and I was gripped by momentary panic. But turns out it was Sharon, who had awakened from deep sleep, saw my hotel number on the dry erase board, and decided she wanted to call me and tell me she loved me. The sound of her voice was like music to my ears, and I was again struck by the feeling that we'd make our way through this.

ᔥ*Chapter Six*ᔥ

Going Home

I am amazed at how quickly a surgery can come and go. Before you know it, you are being discharged from the hospital. I've heard horror stories of hospitals kicking people out as quickly as they could, but Sharon's medical team assured me that two days were all that was required for her to be ready to go home. The doctors came in and gave her a thumbs-up. The nurses did the same and went through the instructions with me on Sharon's care at home. By 11 a.m., we were out the door and heading home. I was hyper-alert to every pothole, sharp turn, traffic and just about everything else, while Sharon was nestled into a pile of blankets in the passenger seat, sleeping off and on. The drive to the ferry and the crossing to the island were uneventful, and by late afternoon Sharon was snuggled comfortably in our guest room, or as I re-named it, "The Recovery Ward." Sharon had been told that the removal of soft tissue is surprisingly not the physical challenge one would think. In fact, she did find that her knee injury had inhibited her mobility far more than the double mastectomy. The psychological issues were much at issue, of course, but Sharon was told that she could carry 10-15 pounds without harm---which she did as she insisted on unloading the dishwasher the first evening home!

Before the surgery and during the pre-op appointments, I was relegated pretty much to being the "second pair of ears" and playing the role of Hoke to Miss Daisy (the driver played by Morgan Freeman, for those not familiar with the movie *Driving Miss Daisy*). But once Sharon was home, I felt that I became a very important part of her recovery. It was my responsibility to make sure she had plenty of drinking water and that she was taking her medications in the correct dosages at correct times (so confusing I had to put it in writing on her nightstand to get the right pills in at the right time). Keeping our cats of 15 years out of the Recovery Ward proved difficult as they both loved to sleep with Sharon, but I managed to run interference each time I opened the door several times a day. I had planned to cook whatever Sharon wanted (and I mean whatever---even if she requested the horrendous smelling turnips and rutabagas she developed a taste for as a child) but fortunately, I only had to reheat food the first week as neighbors and friends brought by meals big enough for the three of us for days. Thank all of you again for that!

While Sharon has a strong stomach for, I think, every vegetable known to man, I have a strong stomach for medical procedures. This came in handy when I performed a vital post-surgical task for Sharon three times a day. Lymph fluid backs up in the tissues in this type of surgery and an unpleasant but necessary post-operative device is needed to take care of the problem. Drains, yes, actual drains are left in place after surgery and these drains need attention three times a day. It was my job to check the drains, "strip" or remove the fluids in the tubing down to the pouches (known as JPs), and empty the JPs and record the amount of fluids on a chart that we'd take back to the doctors for their review. When I got Sharon home, I was able to do the first two drainings awkwardly but successfully while she sat on the bed. The next day, Sharon decided she would watch this process in the bathroom mirror. Sharon had not seen her surgery areas and, until then, had not watched the nurses or me work the tubes on her drains. She was a bit freaked out by the sight, saying she felt like a "Borg" from *Star Trek,* and we tried to laugh about it. But as it turned out, the first sight in the mirror of her breasts and drains after a bit saggy skin-sparing (a good thing) double mastectomy was just too much. It was during this drain check I had my first big scare. She told me she was starting to feel very cold. Our bathroom was admittedly on the cold side and she kept saying, "It's so cold," and she started to shiver a bit. Then she said, "I think I'm blacking out," and sure enough, within seconds, I saw Sharon's eyes roll up into her head. I had to catch her to keep her from hitting the floor and very possibly damaging the delicate stitches. Thankfully we had thought to put a stool nearby where I steadied her and though this relieved my first fear of her injuring herself, a second much worse fear grew as I noticed she had stopped breathing!

Here I am trying to balance her 5' 8" frame on a stool, while holding a drain cup in one hand, the JP in the other and I'm terrified—did she merely pass out or was this something worse? I just kept saying, "You're okay, Sharon, breathe for me. Breathe for me! I have you...." About 10 seconds later (it felt like an hour to me), Sharon took a deep breath and started responding. She actually sounded relaxed when she asked me, "How long was I asleep? It was such a deep, restful sleep...."

I told her she had fainted, and I was so incredibly relieved that she was coherent again. Apparently she did feel rested as she was definitely more relaxed after fainting. I was glad it was at least good for her! Later, she confided in me that, despite the circumstances, it was oddly romantic to wake up in my warm arms, surrounded by my strong embrace. She said it felt so safe. I think my view on the event was markedly different! Anyhow, after that, I decided she wasn't allowed to look at her surgeries in the mirror while I was draining the JPs. I'd never seen anyone faint and stop breathing but I was later told that it was better in that order than to stop breathing and then faint!

After being home for two days, Sharon began taking short walks on our country road. Her body had been through a lot, having been completely free of crutches only a week before surgery (again a timing miracle since she would not have been able to use even one crutch after surgery). All in all, I was amazed at how quickly she recovered.

Two weeks after surgery, we found ourselves in the local clinic to have her JP drains removed (hooray!). Everyone who saw Sharon in town that day remarked how healthy she looked and how amazing it was to see her up and about. I wasn't too surprised at her being up and about though—it's hard to keep Sharon down for long. Go, "Auntie-Oxidant!"

❧Chapter Seven❧

I'm No Hero; Just A Husband

I like to think that when it comes to life-altering events, spouses can rise up to the challenge and do whatever it takes to make the best of the situation. In sadness and trial, I still wanted Sharon happy with me. It helped that Sharon and I have always had a competition when it comes to saying we are in love. It's probably one of the few competitions that is healthy between partners—we say things like "I love you more than you love me" and of course the challenge is on: "I love you infinity plus one" and so on. My apologies to anyone who got sick from that---I'm just a hopeless romantic.

It was during one of the JP checks that Sharon stopped me and declared with a soft yet weighted voice: "You know...you are my hero." I was stunned for a moment and didn't know what to say. I tried to think of some clever retort,

but only could say, "I'm no hero; I'm just your husband."
Afterwards, while Sharon slept, I thought about what she said.
I didn't feel particularly heroic. I just thought I was doing
what I was supposed to do. But it was at that exact moment
that I knew, *I knew* that I was no longer just a spectator in
Sharon's treatment---I was an active participant in making her
better. I was fulfilling the man credo---I can fix this. Well, at
least I could help fix this.

   For months I had felt like a maid, butler, and taxi
driver. All these things that were little things to me turned out
to be big things to Sharon. Sharon has always prided herself
on her independence and, though a very feminine woman, she
also knows how to change the spark plugs and oil in her
vehicles. She often prefers physical jobs in the great outdoors,
and together we have built homes and installed extensive
landscaping. My versatile wife also keeps a beautiful house,
often filled with things she has handmade or re-upholstered.
She wasn't used to being physically dependent on others, but
this was something I could do for her and wanted to do for her.
I relied on my faith that God could and would give me strength
to do the myriad necessary things that I had to do while my
wife recovered. I did more of the odds and ends necessary to
run a household and our set of 16 stairs to the bedrooms began
to show a wear pattern of my footprints! Well, maybe not, but

I began to notice running a household took more little tasks than I knew. I even learned to water houseplants without killing them! Yes, we had said in our vows that we would take care of each other in sickness and in health, but this really can mean becoming an actual personal assistant to an ailing partner. But perhaps it's the little things one can offer to do (or graciously do when asked) that most strengthens the ties that bind.

It wasn't until later I also realized that while Sharon and I had always been close as husband and wife, this ordeal was making us even better friends. I began to see how we had been tested and were being giving the grace to come through with flying colors.

January then became February, and Sharon had to go in for another surgery. It turned out that when the doctors did a closer examination of her lymph nodes, they found a microscopic cancer, a potential time bomb that, undetected, could have caused problems down the road. So Dr. Lee felt that when Sharon came in for her first reconstruction surgery a few weeks later, they would also do a second lymphectomy to see if there were any cancers that had made it past the sentinel lymph nodes known as "gate-keeper" nodes. Her physicians did not expect additional cancers in the lymph nodes but all agreed that subsequent treatment hinged on knowing for sure.

The second surgery felt almost old hat to me. I didn't need the GPS to know where to go this time. The hotel was the same one we had stayed at the first time. I knew where to park, the shortcuts to the hospital, which elevators got us to the right wing (and which hallways got us to the check-in desk!) and which led to the cafeteria. The morning of this multi-task surgery, we were wise to which pastel colored, printed cloth "tent" was the gown and which was the robe, and so forth. (I guess hospitals use printed fabrics for patients to tell the difference between patients and hospital staff, who always seem to get the solid colors!) Once again, I looked for humor when possible and soon we were giggling and doing what I call "church laughing." Both of us were far more comfortable with the pacing and the steps you take from the waiting room to pre-op. The questions weren't so scary and during the wait while Sharon was in surgery, I felt comfortable enough to head back to my hotel room instead of pacing nervously in the hospital waiting room. This go-round, I was better able to predict when the "call" would come and I was able to join Sharon in her recovery room literally five seconds after she arrived. I thought she'd be as alert as she was after her first surgery, but the second surgery was harder on Sharon as they weren't just removing soft tissue. Lymph nodes had been removed, and as part of the reconstruction process, temporary "expanders" had been placed under muscles, sewn directly into the muscle tissues. The expanders would allow the doctors to create large enough pockets for the implants that would come later.

We had already been forewarned that recovery time would be harder so Sharon was given stronger drugs. She slept often and deeply, but not before we got to share a huge sigh of relief that all lymph nodes were cancer free! Besides the obvious relief of catching things as soon as we did, Sharon knew that this also meant that she would not need radiation, and further reconstruction could proceed as planned. Her push for placing expanders in at the same surgery as the second lymphectomy had been a very good decision. Again, after a short stay, Sharon was deemed strong enough to go home, where this round of playing the role of nurse was a bit easier for me, as Sharon only had one JP drain to take care of instead of two.

Before long, it was time to start the expansion process. This would mean a weekly visit to Seattle for about seven weeks and as a result, we got to know her plastic surgery staff well enough to joke freely and swap personal stories from time to time. Sharon would arrive one size and leave the next size bigger on a weekly basis until she arrived at a size she thought went well with her frame. (We likened it to a second puberty but time-lapsed in fast motion!) If I had to miss one of Sharon's expansion appointments, I jokingly sent a "note from home" excusing me from the appointment. Nurse Cheryl, responsible for the expansions, responded a couple of times with a note back lambasting me for my having missed the appointment. She was good at a joke-style guilt trip and the teasing ramped up a few notches from then on. Everyone seemed to enjoy the lighter side of things, I think... especially the patient! I felt that the "harassment" I suffered was worth it if it made Sharon laugh!

Chapter Eight

Chemo Ain't Pretty

Though Sharon was able to avoid radiation by having opted for a double mastectomy rather than lumpectomies, even microscopic involvement in only one lymph node meant that chemotherapy was an advised course of treatment. To accommodate her upcoming chemotherapy during the summer months, my busy work season, I would take a day off to coincide with Sharon's weekly chemotherapy appointment off island.

When I first heard that Sharon was going to have to have six months of chemotherapy, my gut reaction was to think the worst, partly because it sounded so bad, but mostly because I didn't know anything about modern chemotherapy. Sharon's mother had gone through chemotherapy in the early 60s and perhaps that memory influenced Sharon's sister to not have it in the 90s, though the treatment wasn't as harsh and doctors had recommended it.

We learned, as we became more informed on the topic, that research from even just the last few years has made a big difference in how to better tailor the tool of chemotherapy to the individual. Smaller, less broad-spectrum doses can help relieve the well-known side effects of nausea, total hair loss and overall weakness. Therapies are always in review and chemotherapy is under scrutiny as well but it is still favored here in the U.S. for breast cancer patients.

European breast cancer treatments, however, have moved away from chemotherapy in favor of other treatments that have reportedly proven just as successful. Strong intravenous bone-building drugs, called bisphosphonates, have proven in an Austrian study to be on par with chemotherapy for preventing recurrence of breast cancer in the bones, a big problem in Sharon's family. In the U.S., this particular bone-building drug (at this writing) is available only through clinical trials. In lieu of this, Sharon decided that since we don't live in Europe, she would opt for the most statistically tried and true methods currently approved here. The "chemical portion of the plan," as Sharon puts it, would start with chemotherapy and end after five years of hormonal drug therapy in the way of

Tamoxifen or Aromatase inhibitors. Sharon faithfully takes supplements to strengthen bones but she was also very interested in pursuing any FDA approved or trial-based bisphosphonates to strengthen the bones' resistance to cancer as well.

The two oncologists Sharon had spoken with at length at that point guided her decision. Each oncologist has slightly different recommendations to help prevent recurrence and all the information was found to be helpful. We could foresee a time when regular trips to Seattle would not be necessary and were grateful that our insurance would cover a needed interview with a more local oncologist working out of Island Hospital in Anacortes. Happily for me, closer treatment would mean no more eight-lane freeway traffic and downtown Seattle driving for the weekly visits. Our regular 200-mile roundtrip might actually become a mere 40 miles plus the ferry ride.

Sharon's first visit with Dr. Raish, a highly recommended Anacortes oncologist, confirmed an impressive quantity of statistics she had heard: life expectancies jump from a 40% chance of a long life with only surgery to over 80% with chemotherapy as the first part of a five-year pharmaceutical plan to combat recurrence. With microscopic cancer detected only in a "gatekeeper" lymph node, Sharon was a borderline candidate for chemotherapy. Evidence was good that her antibodies were doing what they were supposed to do by attacking and killing cancer in a second node. Chemotherapy was still recommended by both the oncologists Sharon had spoken with at length. Dr. Raish also confirmed that by catching the cancer as early as we did, a plan called "Chemo-Lite" would best suit her situation. Side effects vary among patients but the lower dosages of "Chemo-Lite" minimize the fatigue, nausea and joint aches; hair loss occurs in less than 20% of patients. We learned, to our surprise, that to tell by looking who is and isn't on chemo these days can be impossible.

The recommended time had passed after surgery, and Sharon delayed another week before beginning "Chemo-Lite." She had been back to home-improvement projects with a fury and she didn't relish having to slow down again, but the time couldn't be pushed out much further. Sharon had already been instructed that Chemo-Lite involved a double cocktail of two drugs via an IV drip once a week in Anacortes and she would also take a daily pill (with the required copious amounts of water) for six months. After chemo, Sharon also hoped she could increase her advantages against recurrence by qualifying for the clinical trial in Seattle using the best-known bone-building bisphosphonates. She was willing to try all methods with sound statistics behind them, and anything widely tested and good enough to replace chemotherapy in Europe to prevent recurrence in the bones sounded especially appealing to my wife. The doctor-quoted statement of, "Strong bones resist cancer" resonated loud and clear with Sharon as she had seen breast cancer metastasize into the bones in three of her close relatives.

Of course, drugs trials are multi-purpose with a primary goal often being for FDA approval, but Sharon was willing to be a guinea pig, after hearing nothing but good things about this therapy. Being accepted into the trial program would mean several more months of trips to Seattle but that seemed a small price to pay for even better odds of living a long cancer-free life.

Meanwhile, Dr. Raish was chosen to monitor her chemotherapy for the required six months and would be her doctor for the standard follow-up five years of treatment as well. Best of all, Dr. Raish came highly recommended by many women Sharon knew personally.

In recalling her initial interview with Dr. Raish just weeks after her mastectomy surgery back in January, Sharon reminded me of another set of events that "came knocking."

Three weeks after Sharon's mastectomy, while I was doing my man chores around the home, my back muscles went on strike. The next day, Sharon and our 14-year-old resident niece went off island on a planned shopping trip, Sharon just starting to drive again. The two of them planned to combine her first appointment with Dr. Raish with some needed shopping while I tried a day of bed rest. Our teenage niece would help Sharon with the heavier lifting, such as full shopping bags, and she would get to shop for clothes for her troubles. Well, at the exact time Sharon parked the car for her first appointment with Dr. Raish, my condition worsened. I called from home in excruciating back pain, finding myself unable to move an inch in any direction. So there I was home alone, upstairs, and the only relief I got from searing pain was sitting on the edge of the bed, not daring to move an inch (unfortunately facing the wall instead of the TV) for over six hours. Well, Sharon was so concerned for me that my situation served to get her mind off her own predicament. So even from home, I contributed to helping Sharon keep her mind off her first oncology appointment discussing the dreaded upcoming chemotherapy plan. (What can I say...I had the distraction all planned...right?) Seriously, Sharon was so concerned for me that she even let me interrupt her interview (apologies again, Dr. Raish) when I called her cell phone a second time. I wasn't sure which ferry she was taking but sure was looking forward to getting a glass of water, perhaps some ibuprofen and something to eat. Our closest neighbor at the time was over 1/2 mile away and my manly independent side didn't want to bother friends living 25 minutes away in town...so I waited for my wife. I felt like I was competing in a Survivor-type contest having to balance just so on the edge of the bed for hours. It was that bad. Our poor cats needed to go outside, and finally, I literally crawled down the stairs to let them out. I once had a spinal tap that didn't hurt nearly as bad as this!

Sharon ended up becoming <u>my</u> nurse (as well as a true personal assistant) for the next three weeks when my mobility was severely limited. Whew! When it rains, it pours. I still wonder over another small miracle during this time. Our bedroom television had some issues with the on/off switch— successfully coming on only about half the time and even then it would often shut off unexpectedly. For some reason, for my entire bedroom stay of three weeks, the television set worked flawlessly. It went on the blink again shortly after that. Yet another timing fluke that strikes us as uncanny was that I was rendered pretty much immobile during a very short window when Sharon was in between two surgeries. She had just recovered enough from the first to care for me instead of me for her. For a solid three weeks, I lived in a recliner or its closest relative---a heavily cushioned chair with separate footrest. Stuck in an upright position, I was averaging about 3-4 hours sleep per night, and with my late night TV watching, I got to know every infomercial there was during that time!

The first night I was actually able to sleep in a bed again was at the hotel the night before Sharon's second major surgery, just five weeks after the first one. Whew, that was close! My back did well from then on and I was able to care for her again without a problem. In this life, we will have trouble, but at least the timing allowed one or the other of us to administer needed nursing! I suppose the timing of my immobility made it all the more heartwarming to see how Sharon rallied to immediately switch roles to make sure I was comfortable and well attended to. We're very thankful that at least one of us was healthy enough to take care of the other! This seemed another set of small miracles to us.

During the lull between her second surgery and chemotherapy (a required two month wait), Sharon visited her plastic surgeon once a week for "expansion". As her energy and strength returned, Sharon finally decided to contact her siblings and relay to them her best understanding of both her diagnosis and prognosis. Five months had passed since her diagnosis and she felt better informed and much more confident of a good outcome. In a series of calls, some conference style, she reassured them how good she felt and that she had managed the surgeries well, and that she would soon opt for chemotherapy although she was only a borderline candidate. Because some family members were in disagreement with her decision to choose chemotherapy as part of her treatment, she informed them how important every statistically supported treatment was to her, especially with their family history. She explained to them that she wanted to play it safe in case any microscopic cancer had traveled further. Sharon tried to quell the family fears about chemotherapy, assuring them that she felt confident that methods had improved and that lobbies even as powerful as drug companies could not skew medical data over many decades in matters of such life and death importance without the public at large catching on. Anyhow, her siblings were very glad things weren't worse than they were. Losing one sister two years earlier had been hard enough on all. Sharon was glad for their support but was also glad she had spared them so many traumatic unknowns in the beginning.

I accompanied Sharon to her first chemotherapy session. That day was a particularly busy day for the Cancer Care Center in Anacortes, a quaint town on Washington's scenic coast serving as a big draw for retirees. The paperwork was a bit daunting and an oncology ward presents a whole new set of phrases and terminology to learn. So while Sharon and I both began filling out paperwork to expedite the time, I began doing what I do best---trying to find humor in a tense situation. We discovered that one of the admitting staff, Laura, had also lived in Mississippi, so of course I immediately seized upon "Mississippi" as her new unofficial nickname. The other admitting staff, Kristy, was quickly dubbed "Trouble" as her dry wit so readily found me as an instant target! I suppose I egged her on, especially with her new title, but I knew Sharon was listening and this was my main goal---to lighten the moment.

Soon Sharon was handed a very skinny file folder, a name sticker was placed on her shirt---complete with a personal barcode ID for safety reasons---and we were ushered into THE ROOM. The room for administering chemo was lined with recliners and every chair was filled. Patients were spilling out into the hallway while they waited for an available recliner. Next to each chair was an IV stand, monitors, and other medical equipment. With too few chairs and nurses scrambling to keep up with the workload, that day was particularly hectic for all.

The room was surprisingly loud and Sharon looked understandably nervous. It seemed to her that every patient but her knew what to expect, as there did seem to be a certain routine to all the hustle and bustle. Sharon was a bit timid to study other patients as this seemed like a place one would want privacy. Indeed, some sat with their eyes shut, others knitted, read books, watched portable DVDs or listened to iPods, most off in their own private worlds. I tried to meet the nurses and get to know them to ease the tension, but they were too busy. Sharon was a willing patient, but very nervous about the effects of chemo. Just when she'd start to feel stronger, first from her knee injury and then from surgeries, it was time to take her down a few notches again and she wasn't looking forward to it. The chaos of the first day was an added trial for us as it didn't seem to be a harbinger of easy times to come regarding the six-month-long chemo plan.

Well, when a recliner finally became available, somehow Sharon's veins must have known they faced six months of weekly blood-draws and chemo injections. The late spring day was cold and Sharon's veins retreated from sight from a combination of cold and nerves. The nurses tried to find a proper vein for the chemo IV, but while Sharon was willing, her veins were not. After about a half a dozen pokes, Sharon was becoming the focus of the room. The nurses all seemed surprised that Sharon didn't already have a Portacath installed in the upper chest wall (a small medical appliance that is installed beneath the skin allowing direct vein access). Patients expecting six months of chemo usually appreciate having the device, which sounds scarier than it is. Hardly visible under the skin, the port has a little chamber through which drugs can be injected and blood samples can repeatedly be drawn, a sure vein to access every time after a numbing agent and a quick needle prick. Sharon had inquired about a Portacath before her second surgery, an early but convenient time to get one, but her veins looked fine at that time to the consulting oncologist in Seattle. Her report indeed read that it looked like she would not need one for the upcoming six months of chemotherapy.

As far as determining whether one's veins can stand months of IV injections and blood draws, apparently, looks are deceiving. Sharon's robust-looking veins decided against invasion of any kind on her first day of chemo! Nothing helped her veins "reveal" themselves—not even the warmed blankets, going for a walk, or hot tea. The assessment of not needing a Portacath changed in fast order. During the process of receiving multiple pricks, all Sharon could think of was how she could have avoided another surgery to install the very needed port. Most of all, my very active wife really wanted to avoid another five to six week restriction for lifting after surgery and the fact that two or three days are essentially lost to sleep immediately after surgery, from the side effects of strong painkillers. The prospect of being under anesthesia a third time in four months didn't thrill her either. Her frustration surfaced in the form of steady quiet tears as nurses tried over and over to find a good vein.

Finally, Sharon got hooked up to the chemo drip by way of a baby needle between two knuckles, since the only workable vein was so small. She later laughed with the nurses at how traumatic that first visit was for her and them. She apologized at the time for her tears and explained to the nurses that she mainly wished she'd been better informed about the need for a port ahead of time. Dr. Lee had offered to install a port in February after all, if so requested. In retrospect, perhaps the extra surgery was better than wearing the sometimes uncomfortable device longer than necessary, but Sharon still says she leans to having had a port put in two months early!

We have since learned that between cold weather and nerves, veins can hide from even the best phlebotomists! Chemotherapy itself can be hard on veins and a designated port is very much worth having for anyone facing long-term treatments requiring IVs and weekly blood-draws. To try to make a long story shorter, the lead chemo nurse recognized a real problem and scrambled to get Sharon scheduled for an emergency port-installing surgery before her next chemo the following week. Sharon found herself set up with an emergency consult that she could walk to after her first chemo session, in the same hospital. (Speedy service---thanks to Dorothy, Susan, Enid, Rebecca, Leslie and Carrie and all other nurses there for Sharon that very hectic day and in the following months!)

The consulting surgeon agreed to install a port with, "Can you come back in two days?" Wow, that was fast planning, as surgeries go, and we again marveled at the narrow timing since recovery time couldn't have been cut closer after this surgery for the next planned chemo session. So we gave the ferry service to Anacortes more business that week for Sharon's third surgery. At least this surgery would be a quick one and would solve the "pin the tail on the donkey" approach with her fickle veins to blood-draws and IVs! In trying to get in an IV just before her Portacath surgery, it took another nine needle pricks, including attempts in her hand, elbow, and foot. There were no tears this time, but there might have been a few swear words---but solely at the situation, not toward anyone trying hard to help (and I won't say who said them other than it wasn't me). Even the surgeon had to try several chest locations before finding a vein, but thankfully, that was after Sharon was under anesthesia. It was a steep learning curve for Sharon to discover that even robust veins can play hide and seek when under duress. She counted 23 new holes in efforts to find a vein in all of three days in order for her to receive chemotherapy!

Anyhow, with Sharon's third surgery at 10 a.m., I asked the staff if they thought we'd be able to make the 2:40 p.m. ferry back (it's a direct ferry---much quicker). They didn't think so, but by 11:45, my cell phone rang and the nurses asked me to have the car out front and ready to go—Sharon was "done!" I joked that the surgeon and staff must have a second job at Jiffy Lube since they were so fast. We were back home this time before dark.

The next week when Sharon went in for her chemo, it was a totally different situation. The nurses had time for a bit of casual talk. The room was friendly and relaxed. The labs weren't backed up, and Sharon's port served its appointed function perfectly. She began feeling more at ease that the decision to have chemo was a good one. We settled into a familiar routine of getting up early, catching the 8 a.m. ferry for Sharon's 10:00 lab test appointment, the necessary step before chemo could be ordered and administered. Of course I always stepped inside with Sharon long enough to harass and perhaps flirt a bit with the receptionists and nurses, after which I'd take advantage of being on the mainland to shop for the three of us at home (plus our pets, who possibly would enjoy as much variety as *we* do in our diets if Sharon got her way). I soon got the routine down well enough that I could sneak in lunch at my favorite restaurant in town, and still have Sharon in line for the 2:40 p.m. ferry home.

The weeks began passing (at a slower rate for the patient than for her husband, I'm sure), but the 24 initial chemotherapies became 12 chemotherapies and so on. Sharon's medical folder had grown thick with blood tests and treatment reports but finally, summer was nearing its end and we could see the light at the end of the tunnel. Effects vary quite a bit with each individual, but Sharon's energy levels were down enough that a light exercise routine and basic house chores were challenging enough during the last two months of chemotherapy. The treatment had started to affect her strength and joints, so she avoided tasks such as gardening and playing the piano at this point. We have a big yard that Sharon hand-weeds rather than use herbicides, but she found that some things just had to be postponed or neglected, such as a well-weeded yard. My jobs already kept me busy and Sharon had to accept that no one was going to die from shock of seeing a few healthy weeds amongst the many flowers and shrubs.

Those last few weeks of chemo can seem like a monumental milestone, so during the fourth-to-last visit, I took aside some of the nursing staff and began questioning them about a scheme I had in mind for Sharon's last day. I wanted to do something special (even if it had the distinct possibility of publicly humiliating myself) to commemorate her last chemo. I was worried about being too silly or flippant in the chemo ward, but was assured by all the nurses that something fun would definitely be welcomed.

So I began working in earnest on creating an alter ego that could arrive to surprise and entertain my wife as she sat tethered to an IV stand. Being a child of the 60s and 70s, I fondly remembered a commercial for Fritos featuring an animated character named the Frito Bandito. So my warped mind quickly created the "Chemo Bandito," the unfortunate love child of Frito Bandito & Chiquita Banana. I began sneaking over to the garage at night, telling Sharon I was working out, while in reality I was working on a skit, complete with songs and bad jokes, to perform in commemoration of Sharon's graduation from a six-month stint of chemotherapy. I met with a costumer from our local community theatre, where I had volunteered for years, to help me with a serape (a South of the Border fringed poncho). To complete the ensemble, I began gathering the rest of my gear: long pants (gasp! I have a reputation as being the "guy who always wears shorts"), a rope belt, guitar, sombrero, boots, and spurs. On the morning of her last day, I dropped Sharon off and ran a couple of errands so that I could time Chemo Bandito's arrival while she was in her chair, just before the IV finished but while she was still unable to escape the routine I had planned! I also had a very willing accomplice in our live-in niece, who acted as my sound effect girl by providing the clippity-clop of horse hooves and the jingling of spurs (which turned out to be a handful of bottle caps). Our niece was naively happy to be my willing partner in crime, though she may live to regret it since we have videotape of this day as blackmail material on this young lady if we ever need it!

Well, I have to say the performance went off without a hitch, and I felt good that I had helped Sharon's last day of chemo to have a positive, fun note to end on. I had baked several types of festive looking goodies to be served along the rim of Chemo Bandito's sombrero (sanitarily wrapped in plastic, of course) and all efforts seemed to serve their intended purpose. Both Sharon and I still get a tear in the eye when watching the video...yes, perhaps sappy...but true nonetheless. (Again, I'm told that admitting emotion is the first step to being secure in one's masculinity!) Anyhow, nurses like to take your picture on the last day of chemo and Sharon's picture is easily spotted on the wall, as it is the only one where the patient is wearing a smile *and* a huge sombrero!

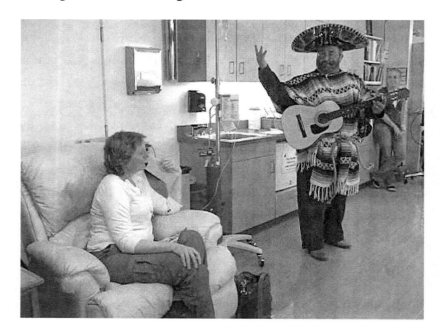

The Arrival of the Chemo Bandito!

Chapter Nine

Cosmetic Surgeries & Clinical "Trials"

Now that the chemotherapy was over, we could focus on the next phase of Sharon's recovery---the final reconstructive surgery. The expanders had done their job and after a few weeks of recovery from chemo, Sharon was allowed to switch out the expanders for a supple set of new-generation silicone implants---something she had been looking forward to for about nine months!

Sharon's surgeon, Dr. Lee, had early on recommended several plastic surgeons, one of whom was Dr. Wandra Miles, whom we had come to visit often for the many weeks required during the preparatory stage for final implants. There had been a several month break in those visits for the duration of chemotherapy but Sharon made an appointment to meet with her plastic surgeon again to plan the final stages of reconstruction. When we first met with Dr. Miles, there was an instant trust. We are able to relate that Dr. Miles is a breast cancer survivor herself, and her easy-going professional manner jelled instantly with both my wife and me. Cheryl, Dr. Miles' lead nurse, especially knew what Sharon needed to hear emotionally early on and we knew from the start that Sharon was in good hands. Throughout the process of reconstruction, we think the staff got a kick out of reminding Sharon that she would always have the breasts of a young woman and that she wouldn't have to have mammograms anymore. Things were sounding better and better.

As touched on before, the first plastic surgery, back in February, had been to place a pair of "expanders" under the breast muscles. The purpose is pretty straightforward. The expanders do just as they suggest—they expand over time to make a muscular cavity for the final implants to reside. The nurse knows exactly where to add more saline, courtesy of a magnetic guide built into the expanders. After seven trips to Seattle for a "fill-up" or "lube and oil," as we sometimes joked, Sharon decided she'd reached the desired limit of her "mid-life adolescent" growth spurt.

Over the months, the upside to having the expanders was they are good at doing their job. The downside was that stretching out the muscle and tissues can be a bit painful and she had to sleep only on her back for over nine months. But my wife endured, knowing that soon they would be removed and the more supple implants would be in.

The upcoming surgery was also a convenient time to take out the Portacath...yet another multiple-task surgery to minimize exposure to anesthesia, recovery times and expense. This surgery was a big occasion for Sharon and me as it meant the surgeries were over. Sharon would soon be visiting her relatives in the Southeast in a few weeks and wanted to look and feel her best. A year had passed since her diagnosis and we found matters infinitely more manageable our second Christmas living with the diagnosis. Sharon soon proved her own comfort level with her new look by wearing anything she wanted—including a plunging neckline swimsuit! All her relatives that Christmas, in fact, couldn't get over that she looked younger and healthier than the last time she had seen them two years before (despite her six month stint on chemotherapy).

Speaking of Sharon's relatives, her family history served as a regular reminder of the fate three close relatives had experienced when the breast cancer had spread to the bones. So Sharon was still very interested in a clinical trial coming up shortly after her last plastic surgery that used Austrian-tested bisphosphonates that seemed particularly adept at helping bones resist cancer. Well, Sharon had been the beneficiary of uncanny speediness in receiving care in some cases, as mentioned, but she had also experienced freakish delays in other instances.

Getting the interview with the physician for the clinical trial would prove to be of the freakish delay sort. We drove to Seattle the night before, staying at a hotel so as to accommodate the early morning appointment at this highly esteemed cancer treatment facility---a facility we had supported by contributions years before Sharon's own diagnosis. Well, Sharon was checked in, complete with a hospital-type identity armband, and then was interviewed and examined in an hour-long session with the physician who would oversee her in this clinical trial if she qualified. In this interview, Sharon was encouraged with the news that she was the perfect candidate and the doctor would love to have her participate in the trial. Again, she was told that European research documented that the drug was on par with the benefits of chemotherapy to combat recurrence. All this was very appealing, as you might imagine, especially since Sharon had been told that treatments are cumulative in their ability to combat recurrence. I sat in another part of the building while

Sharon was examined and the next thing I knew was that my wife was on her cell phone, calling me in tears. At the last moment, the physician looked at her paperwork and in shocked surprise had informed Sharon that she was very sorry, but due to a clerical error on their office's part, Sharon could not qualify. She was two weeks too late from her last chemotherapy. Sharon had actually been sent the paperwork from this facility after the deadline had already passed. She had once again slipped through the cracks of administration. The doctor did tell Sharon that her oncologist in Anacortes could treat her with a similar drug called Zometa, which also builds bones, but the best proven drug would not be available to her. My dear wife, hopeful of yet another hedge against recurrence, only heard in essence: Due to our mistake, you no longer qualify. Go home and settle for an inferior drug treatment.

Well, suffice it to say that this was the low point in her experience with the medical system but because of a letter Sharon wrote to this facility, the top brass called her personally and apologized, as well as wrote her, explaining: "Because of your feedback, we identified the following needed improvements: 1) "The Research Integration Manager will work with Intake management to make sure research personnel are utilized appropriately and 2) Training will be provided to increase skills in communicating with patients about clinical trial eligibility."

After all this, somehow we were still billed for the appointment. Sharon responded that they should be paying our hotel and travel expenses, but at the very least should not charge us for that appointment! Apparently, the top brass agreed as another letter was soon sent that removed all charges. We do wish all patients in this trial the very best and hope to hear that all goes well enough to have the European bisphosphonates version approved soon in the United States. We can't help but wonder, at this writing, if the workload and available doctors and medical support staff---including insurance personnel---will improve or worsen in the future with new legislation regarding medical coverage in the U.S.A. The bottom line is we all want fast yet thorough care. We hope that with whatever legislative changes are made, access and management of health care only gets easier for both patients and doctors and their supporting staff. This is a tall order. Sharon is hopeful that medical insurance opportunities will broaden, as she saw how her sister's insurance was tied to her employment. The funny thing is...you can't work when you get really sick! And COBRA insurance isn't affordable for most after a job loss. Medical costs have soared into the stratosphere...falling far from the ideal goal of affordable medical coverage, regardless of employment or pre-existing conditions. Perhaps if the government is going to spend big bucks on something for its citizens, medical care should be a high priority since many find adequate insurance too costly. Perhaps better affordability needs to be addressed by a combination of things (maybe having insurance companies compete across state lines is one of those things) but it looks like legislation is definitely needed to build an infrastructure to solve the problem...but I digress, as this is not a political book by any means!

Chapter Ten

Living After The Diagnosis

As of this writing, it has been almost three years since my wife got that harrowing confirmation of breast cancer. It is with relief that I write now that though for two years, Sharon was under the belief that she had had Stage Two breast cancer, another review of her lab work from the double mastectomy indicated that a lab technician had made a mistake in totaling the sizes of the tumors removed. In fact, now we are told that Sharon's cancer had only been Stage One all along! The course of treatment, based on other data at the time, would have been the same, but wow...that would have been great to have caught earlier...but better late than never!

Of course there are worse fates such as longer and more chronic illnesses than what has faced us at this point in life. We are grateful in so many ways and strive to look at this experience for what can be learned from it to help us, and others in the long run. Sharon says that she has employed many ways to keep the harder aspects of her experience in perspective. I remember early on in our experiences with chemotherapy that Sharon told me that to keep her chemotherapy experience in perspective, she kept in mind her friends who experienced as much or more discomfort for the sake of carrying a child for 9 months; and that it was strange how some of the symptoms were actually somewhat similar. Experiences vary, of course, but the nausea, joint aches and need for bed-rest reminded her of friends who had experienced moderately difficult to difficult pregnancies. Of course, the circumstances vastly differed as Sharon was not expecting a new life but was trying to save her own.

Thankfully, I've only faced brushes with my mortality via car and motorcycle accidents. Both times, I walked away only limping a bit but by the condition of the vehicles, both deemed totaled at first, I should have been in the hospital. But as a breast cancer patient, my wife faced a much more enduring and serious scenario. Sharon told me something one day that struck a very vivid image in my head. She said that, in the midst of treatments, she felt a bit braver to remember soldiers who volunteer daily to face physical impairment and mortality by serving in war zones; and while theirs is a chosen job, it's a job that involves laying life and limb on the line in defense of others. Their bravery served to inspire her to get through a difficult time.

When I look back on the last two years, I see so many caring doctors, nurses, support staff, and friends and family who were there for us. The fact is, we were both so overwhelmed by the situation that at times we were like zombies just going from point A to point B and hoping for the best. Both of us had to be willing to rely on others as never before.

Anyone with a life-threatening cancer diagnosis will inevitably have to go from one enormously trying unknown to another, especially during the initial diagnosis process, which often takes weeks, if not months, to determine the extent of the problem. Along the way, we shared lows that made us feel like we were in a bottomless pit, but we also had moments of elated relief, tenderness and awe. To find out that the disease is treatable in the majority of cases like hers---this was definitely a high! It is now often said that early stage breast cancer is an "ailment." While very serious, it need not be a death sentence. We are encouraged that scientists continue to work hard to find treatments and earlier ways to diagnose the problem and, best yet, ways to prevent it altogether!

We remember that even through the roughest times, it was important to leave room for pleasant surprises. The kindness of strangers came into play for us, such as a former breast cancer patient who, although they had never met, offered Sharon the use of her vacant home only a mile from the Anacortes hospital anytime we needed on our weekly chemo trips off island. And of course there was the ferry captain who turned the boat around for Sharon. We still marvel at that "turn of events" with smiles on our faces. And we will always be thankful for the outpouring of caring, prayers, and hope. We saw thoughtful and kind acts of outreach such as the "care baskets" put together by volunteers from Swedish Medical Center for newly diagnosed cancer patients; or the creative handmade lap quilts offered to each Island's Hospital chemo patient, made by an Anacortes sewing circle who call themselves the "Chemo Rippers." We found out about many support groups for cancer patients, ranging from grass-root gatherings to formal support-group chapters organized by the American Cancer Society. In some cases, some of these organizations are able to provide lodging near hospitals for out-of-town patients and families. In any case, we concluded that even independent types, such as Sharon, can benefit from the strength and perspective of those who have survived cancer treatment and "paying it forward" is the hope for this book as well.

We had always heard that priorities change around having faced a life-threatening situation and we see how this is true in our case as well. Getting and staying healthy is a constant motivation to stick to an exercise plan and a low-fat diet---rich in anti-oxidants, of course! We've taken an additional step of growing our own organic vegetables. Working the garden beds in the fresh air and sunshine is probably as good for us as the food produced. Perhaps most importantly, our increased awareness that time is short (even for the longest-lived of us) has Sharon and me talking and doing more to help others. Again, the hope is that our humble story contained in this book will make the complete unknowns seem less daunting for those who are just beginning this journey.

A common theme running through our story has been the help we received to combat this disease. The medical staff, with their knowledge, patience and outright kindness, made Sharon wish she had gone into the field of medicine. It's a noble calling and too few are entering this field. The fact that doctors and nurses can be so strong in the face of life-threatening situations, or worse, is nothing less than inspiring.

With a cancer diagnosis, one has to prepare to be very brave. Sharon knew she had to examine more than ever before what would make her strong in facing the journey before her. She was forced to search her soul and her faith to get through the experiences of battling a life-threatening cancer that has taken several relatives. For Sharon, a deep sense of dependency was new for her, other than the familiar comfort of our marriage and her faith. Now in case you didn't think this book covered enough private stuff already, here comes the really personal stuff! If you think that faith has no place in a book like this, then you should probably skip the next section.

When Sharon didn't feel the strength to face the situation alone, two constants sustained her. First was our love and commitment for each other to stick it out together *no matter what*. I will do anything for Sharon, and she knows it. But while I can repair a broken chair or offer a shoulder to lean on, major medical and spiritual matters are way beyond my ability to fix. And getting a diagnosis of cancer surely qualifies as a motivation to question faith, and even to question God. This is why Sharon and I also share a strong commitment to understand that while God does not always spare us from trouble in this life, there is an ultimate thread for good running through a world that seems caught between paradise and complete disaster. Things happen in our lives from time to time that can make us question the meaning of our lives, and what our purpose is here? For both Sharon and myself, our comfort often came from faith that the God we believe in is not the author of evil, and that *whatever* appears as meaningless and a true waste of personal potential *can* truly be redeemed by a God that, "can work all things together for good."

Cancer is the just the kind of thing that makes one question the meaning of life and what comes after this life. Sharon likes to say that when it comes to experiences of loss, God is the universe's greatest recycler! He can "re-purpose" any bad experience for good." Both Sharon and I have also long believed that life continues beyond the grave and that there is more to the meaning of life than the self-defined meaning that departs with each of us when we die. Circumstances from the age of three had shown Sharon that even exceptionally kind and good mothers can be wrenched from their children, creating an aching absence that would cause her to question "why?" for the rest of her life. When moments of overwhelming doubt worked past her overall faith, Sharon would retreat to the "Recovery Room" and read the Psalms of David and anything she could get her hands on to better reveal a God who cares and one who has actually shared in our sufferings.

Some say that science and faith are not compatible. We don't buy that, especially when it comes to treatment for the critically ill. Sharon says she needed both science and faith to get through her experience with a life-threatening cancer. She is inspired by faith in a Creator-God that precedes the billions-of-years-old universe that we see, and that upon further investigation, has declared the infinite value of each individual. What better foundation, she asks, is there for hope despite our immediate difficult circumstances? Whether our problems are man-made or a random glitch in nature, I agree with Sharon in that I hope God doesn't see fit to test us on this scale for a long time to come! Some may perceive even a faith as basic as this as subversive, silly or something that weakens one's resolve to be a self-made, strong individual. From our experience, it's doubt that made us pale in the face of difficulty, not faith. Faith is like a house foundation---you don't always see it or know that it is there, but it is what supports the house through storms, sunny days, and even the occasional earthquake. And the stronger the foundation, the sturdier the rest of the house remains.

When we first got the confirmation of Sharon's breast cancer, our niece (who had moved in two years before with us because she lost her mother to breast cancer) wrote on a

111

colorful card several quotes from the Bible. We put her card on the refrigerator to see every day. Sharon and I both referred to them when feeling down and needing a bit of strength. I will paraphrase them here:

For I will restore your health and your wounds I will heal, says the Lord. Jeremiah 30:17

God is faithful and will not let you be tested beyond your strength. 1 Corinthians 10:13

I wrote one more passage on a chalkboard hanging in our dining area that spoke to my wife (and is also the basis of one of my favorite songs by U2):

He lifted me out of the pit of despair, out of the mud and the mire. He steadied me and set my feet on solid ground.

Psalms 40:2

And perhaps because Sharon lost so many of her family in the prime of their lives, Sharon's favorite verse is *Isaiah 54:17* which says,

No weapon forged against you will prevail...

These strong words of comfort strengthen Sharon still. She embraces these words to mean that even though our bodies are not free from the assault of illness or cruelty of one sort or another, there *is* hope because death is the ultimate weapon *only* to the temporary housing of our spirits---the fragile and mortal body---and we are doing all we can to take care of that!

It is with delight that I report that Sharon is doing amazingly well. Her blood tests have all been great and she's feeling strong---the key, she says to not feeling like a patient anymore. She's looking and feeling younger between almost daily workouts and lots of anti-oxidants (after all, she has to live up to her name of Auntie-oxidant)!

Friends and family tell Sharon how amazing she looks and I tell her this all the time as well because it is true. Yes, she has been challenged in ways she never would have chosen, but having faced her own mortality in the prime of her life, she has become a stronger person. She says there is too much to be done here yet and has searched for clearer meaning and purpose to each day. She gives more of her resources and time to others, and is pursuing the completion of her own novel that has been in the works for years. She has also thrown herself into improving her piano skills so as to "comfortably" play in public. (She recently had one public appearance at the keyboard, but says that the first time was only practicing so that one doesn't count!)

Sadly, Sharon's three favorite "chemo buddies" are no longer with us. Lung, stomach and prostate cancers were too far along to reverse. They are missed, and are more reasons why we have become very involved with the American Cancer Society's Relay for Life in our community.

While the specter of cancer will undoubtedly linger as a haunting presence in our minds, we know that there are researchers working tirelessly to find a cure, and not just for breast cancer. I felt motivation enough to start a Relay team of our own to raise money for research and support of cancer patients. I've enjoyed also becoming part of the Steering Committee as the Sponsorship Chairman for the local chapter of Relay for Life. We have laughed and hugged survivors, and have offered a shoulder and a willing ear to those just starting their fight. Being a part of Relay for Life has also given me a greater appreciation for how even a community as small as ours can still make a difference. Let me extend thanks here for the "Tenacious Trek Trackers," or "T-3," who walk for a cure in our local relay every summer. Thanks, team, for all your support---it means more to Sharon and myself than you will ever know!

As a result of this years-long journey, both of us have forged new friendships amongst other survivors and medical personnel. Sharon's cancer has changed both of us. It has made us more aware of the preciousness of life and of the importance of not taking each other for granted. We are more disgustingly, openly "googly-eyed" for each other than ever! To this day, just thinking about my wife hearing her diagnosis alone without me puts a lump in my throat. We want to be around a while yet, so both of us are paying greater attention to being active and eating---yes, really---those six to nine servings of fresh healthy produce each day, even if it's via blender!

Lastly, we're confident that Sharon's oncologist closely follows the latest research. She is indeed getting intravenous Zometa treatments every six months, for two more years, which contributes to even greater odds that she will never have a recurrence of breast cancer in the bones, which appears to be a trend in her family. We try to follow the latest advice that helps patients do their part too in preventing recurrence. Sharon has adopted several lifestyle changes to help decrease inflammation in the body, a problem that can contribute to cancer-susceptibility. Patients can do a lot too to improve the odds, including: Alternative exercises, which facilitate relaxation and deep breathing, with active weight-bearing exercises, and exercise at least three hours a week---but preferably daily! Get lots of fresh produce and fresh air. Maintain a high-fiber/low fat diet, limit sugar and caffeine, and take calcium and vitamin D supplements to improve the immune system---all things Sharon has incorporated in her new and improved lifestyle.

There is much advice out there and what we have learned is that the patient must be proactive and assertive to discover and take advantage of every chance for better care. Sometimes that care is self-regulated by starting healthier lifestyle habits and by way of the dreaded breast self-exam. Sharon herself had missed the slight dimpling effect on the underside of her size DD breast, as had her gynecologist, a few weeks prior to her diagnosis. Again, another reason to be well informed, and to do frequent and thorough breast self-exams— not just in the shower, but in a mirror as well. Sharon says, "Inform yourself and do all the routine checks. Yes, it's scary but just do it!

As we look forward on the medical front, new and more efficient and cheaper diagnostics are in research and development all the time. Sharon found out that medical appointment schedulers, least of all, are aware of the latest diagnostic tools, and they are almost always in a hurry. If you are in a high-risk family for breast cancer, or any other cancer, her advice is to be even more assertive in knowing what prevention advice is out there and what diagnostics are available. The tide of understanding and treating breast cancer is turning, especially when cancer is caught early!

As for me...life after my wife's diagnosis of cancer has motivated me to improve my awareness of "health tactics." I'm eating more veggies as well and am trying to keep to an exercise routine. I'm more aware that life is short and I feel extra motivation to help others; but most importantly, I appreciate every day I get to spend with a most incredible woman whom I call my "Precious Gift Of God." (And now the secret is finally out as to the meaning of the introductory dedication given to Sharon...my PGOG.)

ᴖ*Chapter Eleven*ᴣ

Epilogue

When I first sat down to write this book, I did so as a bit of personal therapy. I also wanted to chronicle our experience of dealing with the diagnosis and treatment stages, for those as overwhelmed as us at the immensity of such a journey. My intention also was to connect with other men who love the women in their lives and find themselves facing a similar situation. As the pages added up, I realized that this was an opportunity to reach out to other couples just starting down their path of dealing with breast cancer. This was a chance to "pay it forward," and again, I hope our story has given a bit of helpful information, a glimmer of hope, maybe a laugh or two and encouragement to seek all the support one can.

Sharon and I ultimately believe that we have reason to face trials with dignity, that pain and loss *can* actually be only temporary setbacks. It can be very difficult to "wait and see" how all can work together for a higher purpose but the best we can do for each other is to just keep trying to apply that faith in every circumstance. This is the challenge and suffice it to say that, *"...Thy will be done on earth as it is in heaven"* continues to get a lot of play in our lives. We hope our readers will find peace and strength in this book as it is likely that many of you who had read this far have been compelled to do so by perhaps very harsh personal circumstances of your own. The point is to find strength where you can and know that *you are not alone*.

We all have our "toolbox" of resources to help us through a trial like breast cancer. The following suggestions might be helpful "tools," universal to all: Once you have a diagnosis, a virtual deluge of information and appointments will soon follow. A day planner will come in handy for keeping track of appointments, often weeks or months out; and a calendar of some sort is helpful in keeping track of medications. Get yourself a binder where you can keep receipts and documentation. Another section of your binder should be notebook paper---keep it handy for phone conversations with doctors or insurance companies--- conversations that are always guaranteed to be a bit technical.

You can keep a diary there too (in case you decide to write a book).

Rather than falling into assuming the worst financial scenario, talk to your insurance company early on. They may cover more than you think. In any case, find out what your coverage is and what your expenses might be. Will it cost you more to see a doctor out of your preferred area? Maybe for some, a voice recorder might be appropriate to record questions to ask at a later date, or to record what you are being told so you can listen to it again at a later time. And don't forget the power of the Internet. There is a lot of information out there covering everything from basic medical research and advice (again, www.breastcancer.org was helpful to Sharon) and one can also search for organizations and foundations that can assist with financial support. Some drug companies provide discounts and hospitals may have a liaison to help arrange for medication discounts. My friends and family were some of the most important "tools" in my tool chest. So many people offered a word of encouragement, advice to help out when I needed it (and when Sharon needed it too). The home-cooked meals after Sharon's initial surgery still bring warm memories. And of course, my walk with God strengthened me so many times when I was feeling low or powerless to help.

You Can't Fix Everything

A word from Sharon:

I heard some good advice recently in passing: Don't let a rough patch in life define the rest of your life. We don't know what we will face but whatever it is, a posture of assuming the worst robs us of any potential peace and joy. When facing great trial, one needs a source of hope more than ever.

Receiving a cancer diagnosis has compelled me to better understand: Is there a sure source of love, joy, peace, and goodness that I can actually hope for? (I quote Galatians, chapter five in part here.) Somehow I just don't think that these things are an invention of us creatures of dust. I've found out a little too well that our bodies are made of dust; that's for sure. I can doubt my faith with the best of them at times (as the strains of "Dust in the Wind" run through my head) but I finally have to ask: What makes life worth fighting for? The above list of attributes comes to mind and since my diagnosis, I know that I have seen these characteristics more than ever in the medical profession, in friends and family and most of all in my husband.

I have many people to thank for helping me through some of the most difficult moments of my life: all the doctors and staff named in this story, and many more unnamed among friends and relatives. But most of all, the person I must thank is my amazing husband, who has a talent for laughing and living large that he thankfully shares with me on a regular basis! His presence often made a huge difference for me and I admit that my hardest moments coincided (somehow) with the times when he was not there, right beside me. In hindsight, we could have accommodated that better, but it was I who thought I had a handle on things more than I did a time or two when, instead, I found myself inconsolable for a brief time. I'm very thankful to have a husband with a strong protector and provider instinct who wouldn't put up with that for long! He truly found ways to help "fix it," in his stubborn wife's case...mainly by lending me his supportive presence. Even a mere willingness to be there when I insisted, "Nah, I'm good," was a big help! I admit to needing his faith, optimism and strength of character more than I ever thought I would! (The now permanent mascara stains still on one of his favorite t-shirts attest to that!)

Through all this, I'd never felt more loved than during the events that threatened my life, incapacitated me physically from time to time, and disfigured me to an extent that has been remedied more than I thought possible. And through it all he maintained that no matter what, he found me attractive! That's love! I'm humbled by being so cared for, that's for sure! I'd

You Can't Fix Everything

like to think that overcoming the struggles in life boils down to one thing…as my husband wrote in an earlier chapter: "Love gives us wings!"

Sharon & I return to the spot where our lives became one at the Outdoor Chapel. Camp Olympia, 2008

Epilogue

****

This letter appeared in Island Hospital's *Heartbeats Magazine*, Fall of 2008; a letter Sharon wrote to Dr. Raish and all the support staff at her last chemotherapy.

To the Oncology (Cancer Care) Staff:

A lot can be said about helping the needy.... Well, I found myself as one of the needy with a cancer diagnosis at age 49. If I had known of all the advances in science and kind faces involved in this journey, I would not have dreaded it so. I've also been amazed with the dignity and concern of other patients. It's pretty rarefied air in a place where people are facing their mortality and the thinker in me is greatly intrigued by what sustains our spirits through such trying times.

My best-going theory is that there is an angelic impulse within us to help each other in times of need. I think such actions bear witness to the source of all things good.

The time you all have taken, the dedication and sincere concern... you will not be forgotten. I won't miss the place, but I will miss the people! Thanks for helping me with a second chance...I will sure try to make the best of it.

God Bless You All

Author's Note: 50% of all profits from the sale of this book will go to cancer research and treatments.

Please feel free to share your comments with us by visiting our website:

http://youcantfixeverything.blogspot.com/

Email: johnandsharonboyd@gmail.com

The greatest day of my life,
April 14, 1990!

San Diego, 2010; Celebrating
Our 20th Anniversary!

Our cousin Seth Cook taught us time and time
again that life is too short to take seriously!

You Can't Fix Everything

CPSIA information can be obtained at www.ICGtesting.com
Printed in the USA
LVOW071543030113

314244LV00017B/664/P